The Future Firefighter's Preparation Guide

Be The Best Firefighter Candidate You Can Be!

Steve Prziborowski

ISBN: 978-1-4834-0423-3 (sc)
ISBN: 978-1-4834-0422-6 (e)

Lulu Publishing Services rev. date: 12/09/2013

Dedication

This book is dedicated to the men and women who are fortunate enough to serve in the fire service – currently, in the past, and in the future.

To my wife Bonnie, thank you for your endless love and support and for allowing me to do all that I do.

To my long-time friends Greg Vitz, Andy Pestana, and Ron Phillips. All three of you were there with me from the beginning, when I officially started the long haul to become a firefighter. The three of you were and still are a great support network.

To all of the mentors who have assisted me and guided me throughout the years in my pursuit of being the best I can be. There are so many individuals to mention, but you hopefully know who you are and how much you mean to me.

To the fire service, my other family, thank you for giving me a career I can sincerely be proud of, and that I immensely love and value. I don't take for granted what I am so fortunate to do every day. I am forever grateful and humble to have the opportunity to provide courtesy and service to the communities, the department, and the personnel I am fortunate enough to protect and to serve.

To the future firefighters reading this book, I hope this inspires you and challenges you to be the best you can be both now and in the future. More importantly, I hope it helps you get the opportunity to call yourself a firefighter. As you become successful in your career pursuits, please don't forget to pay it forward and help those that were once like you and I – future firefighters!

Table of Contents

Foreword

On August 16, 1985, I was mowing the lawn at my parents' house when the local fire chief pulled up in his pick-up and asked me, "When are you going to join the fire department?" At sixteen, I was still in high school and still very uncertain about my future career endeavors.

Persuaded by the brief conversation, later that night, I attended the monthly business meeting at the local volunteer firehouse. Sitting in the back of the apparatus bay, I filled out an application and was immediately issued a set of turnout gear and a Motorola pager. In a matter of minutes, I became a probationary member of the Wilder (KY) Volunteer Fire Department.

Growing up, I spent countless hours/days/nights at the firehouse where my dad served as a volunteer firefighter and eventually as fire chief. As a young child, the time I spent at the firehouse was filled with adventure and excitement. Bright red trucks, tons of chrome, big boots and oversized helmets—the firehouse was a child's paradise. But the time commitment and personal sacrifice required of my dad over the years had taken its toll on my mom and our family as a whole.

When I returned home after attending the meeting that night, I informed my mom that I had joined the fire department. She was less than pleased. In fact, when the pager went off just a few hours later, she refused to let me go. After a brief debate, I asked her, "What if everyone's mother held their son back from becoming a firefighter— who would help those in need?" From that night on, my mother has been one of my strongest supporters and has never again questioned my career choice.

Two years later, I would be graduating high school and venturing out on my own. If you were to ask my parents at that time if they thought I would go to college and pursue higher education, I'm certain they would've responded with a very assertive, "Hell no!"

Much to my parents' surprise, I graduated high school and went off to pursue a bachelor's degree in fire science. Six years later (yes, I loved it that much), I had earned bachelor degrees in Fire Administration and Arson Investigation and an associate's degree in Emergency Medical Care from Eastern Kentucky University.

With degrees in hand and several years of volunteer/paid experience under my belt, I was ready to begin my career as a full-time, paid firefighter.

Unfortunately for me, *The Future Firefighter's Preparation Guide* was not in existence at the time. My path to becoming a career firefighter included a slew of mistakes, countless days of testing and untold dollars spent on postage and road miles to cover my travels to testing sites throughout the country.

In short, I had the passion and the dedication to be a firefighter, but I was blinded by the expectation that because I had an education and some experience, the door of opportunity would automatically be opened for me. Nothing could have been further from the truth.

The Future Firefighter's Preparation Guide is a much-needed text for the next generation of fire service leaders. Chief Prziborowski's years of experience as a career firefighter, chief officer and instructor are evident in his plainspoken, straightforward approach in preparing and educating the next generation of fire and emergency service professionals.

The fire service is a profession with longstanding traditions (red trucks, loud sirens, fire poles, etc.), some of which will remain the signatures of our profession, while others will eventually fade into the past. Our profession is changing at an incredibly fast pace and those who will successfully fill our ranks in the future will likely be required to endorse and pursue change at an unimaginable rate.

Gone are the days of the checkerboards and park benches in front of fire stations. Sweat and soot-covered faces are no longer the image of bravery. Today's firefighter is a physically fit, compassionate, blue-collar technician, who carries the education and training credentials of a white-collard professional. On rare occasions we are asked to take extraordinary risks to save the life of another, but more frequently, we are asked to extend a helping hand to a less fortunate citizen in need.

To be frank, your choice to become a "firefighter" is admirable and will without question be recognized and appreciated by the citizens you will eventually serve. If your choice to pursue this profession is with the hopes and dreams of becoming a "hero," this is NOT the career for you. A true firefighter is someone who exemplifies the passion and dedication of a humble public servant. Your actions as a firefighter at times will undoubtedly be labeled by some as heroic, but it's your humility and dedication to being the best you can be that will ultimately bring you success.

I wish you the best in your career endeavors as a firefighter and future leader of the fire service. I encourage you to take the advice offered within this text and share the dream that I have shared for the last 27 years—the dream of saying, "I'm a firefighter."

Good luck—stay safe!

Timothy E. Sendelbach
Editor-in-Chief
FireRescue Magazine

Preface

Why another firefighter preparation book you might ask? There are a handful of firefighter preparation books, but most of them seem to focus on a specific area, such as the written examination or the oral interview. I wanted to create a one-stop book that expanded on how you, the future firefighter, can help prepare yourself to be the best you can be!

While this book may seem that it was written for a firefighter candidate in California, it really was not. My intention was for this information to benefit any future firefighter, regardless of where they live or plan to work. Realize though that some of the terms and requirements can and do change from state to state; however, the overall theme and concepts should remain constant throughout the United States. I will try to make specific references and notations when possible, that will help clarify any differences.

For specific information related to the firefighter hiring process, including valuable tips and suggestions to ensure you score the best you can, I encourage you to visit my website at www.chabotfire.com

Introduction

What – me become a firefighter? Of course! When I was a little child, like many other children, I wanted to become a fireman when I grew up (I say fireman not to be politically incorrect, but to use a term that was still appropriate in the 1970's). As long as I can remember, I enjoyed having my father take my by fire stations, either in my hometown, or when we drove by one in the course of our travels. This fascination or dream doesn't always continue for every child. Many of them lose this fascination around the time they reach their teenager years, when they have other priorities such as girls, cars, friends, and sports (in no specific order).

I was one of those children that never lost that fascination with the fire service. Even as a teenager enjoying those things other teenagers do, I remember still enjoying visiting fire stations. Even in Junior High School and High School, I remember going to my neighborhood fire station (San Leandro Fire Station #1, now Alameda County Fire Station #9) and just hanging out with the firefighters and trying to just soak up the environment and learn anything I could.

While I did not get the chance to actually ride on the fire apparatus, I did enjoy hearing the calls come in and seeing the rigs leave with their lights and sirens on as well as discussing the calls after the crews returned. There were a few family friends that worked for the fire department and I used to enjoy talking with them whenever I could about their jobs, and also visiting them when I could at the fire stations.

Immediately after high school, I enrolled at California State University Hayward, with the intent of someday being a firefighter, but not taking it as seriously as I should have. I remember even toying with the idea of taking some fire technology classes at the local junior college (Chabot College in Hayward) while I was working on my four-year degree; however, that never panned out, probably for the better given my age, level of maturity, and level of motivation at the time.

While working on my four-year degree (which I really wasn't sure what it was going to be in – I was still somewhat undecided), I was also working full-time at Longs Drugs Stores, as a member of their management team. While being a manager at Longs Drugs (now CVS) might not seem glamorous (trust me, it wasn't), it did provide decent pay and benefits, and also valuable customer service and work experience for the resume and for the future. Plus, there was a great bunch of people to work with, which made it fun and worthwhile.

As I was getting close to finishing up my four-year degree at California State University Hayward, it was getting clear that I did not want to spend the rest of my life working at the drug store, and/or in the retail trades. I remember one of my fellow managers telling me a story about a golf game he had recently played. He was paired with a business person that was telling him about all of the exciting deals he had made the previous day and all the manager could think of from the previous day was the display of feminine hygiene products he had created. He had laughed, saying that was the highlight of his day (sarcastically of course). That pretty much sealed it for me, as I didn't want to be in the same position.

My best friend Greg Vitz (now a Captain with the Stockton Fire Department) was also working at Longs with me and was also finishing up his college education at the same college as I was. He also had an interest in the fire service since he was a small child as well. In fact when we were both in high school, I remember looking at Firehouse Magazine and admiring and discussing the work of a firefighter. One day at lunch while working at Longs, we both seemed to agree that we needed to start focusing on a career in the fire service, especially after realizing how mundane and limiting a career in retail would be for us.

Upon graduating from Cal State Hayward, both of us immediately enrolled at Chabot College, in their Fire Technology program, to work towards our two-year degree and start the process of becoming a firefighter. We graduated Cal State Hayward in December 1990 and were enrolled in the next available quarter, the spring quarter beginning in April of 1991. We also started to take entry level firefighter exams at local fire department, even before we started the college program, providing us with a valuable way of getting our feet wet and exposing us to what we were getting into. While I failed my first written test with the City of Hayward in January of 1991, I made a point to not let that ever happen again. Within a couple of months, I was taking the City of San Jose's test, and I ended up getting a score of 95% and ranking in the top 50 (out of thousands of candidates).

Greg and I put together our plan – to take as many tests as we qualified for and to get our EMT and Firefighter 1 Certificates as quickly as we could, finish up our two-year degrees in Fire Technology as quickly as we could, and hopefully get hired in a couple of years. Like many candidates, we felt we could get firefighter jobs within a year or two. Boy, were we in for a surprise.... If all else failed, we figured we would look at paramedic school, knowing that a paramedic license would greatly increase our chances of getting hired and narrow our pool of competitors. We were correct.

While at Chabot College, we met two other serious candidates (Ron Phillips, now an Engineer with the Sacramento Metropolitan Fire District; and Andy Pestana, now an Engineer with the South San Francisco Fire Department). The four of us started taking tests around the state and did what we could to better ourselves, to help increase our odds of getting hired.

Well, while all of us were scoring highly on our firefighter examinations, and also getting interviews with the fire chiefs (going about as high as you can go, short of getting a job offer), we just weren't getting those conditional job offers. Upon completion of our two year degrees at Chabot, including our EMT and Firefighter 1 certificates, Greg and I knew we had to find a paramedic school to go on to. The hard part was that Greg and I were both working full-time as managers at Longs Drugs, and also living on our own, away from our parents (the American Dream, so to speak).

We realized we couldn't do paramedic school and still work full time. We actually decided to step down from our full-time jobs, to work part-time and have time to go to paramedic school, take tests, and do what we had to do to become full-time firefighters. This resulted in about a $20,000 a year pay cut, and having to move back home with our respective parents to help save money. Not the thing someone wants to do, especially after having lived on his or her own for a few years. Oh well, we do what we have to do to get ahead in life.

We found a paramedic school in the Sacramento area, and started commuting two days a week, leaving five days in the week to work part-time, take firefighter tests, volunteer, and study for paramedic school. To me, paramedic school was the toughest undertaking I had ever done; tougher than competing my four-year degree.

During this time, I was also participating in the Student Firefighter Work Experience Program through Chabot College, riding along with the Oakland Fire Department. I was assigned to a certain shift and station and I could ride along as a Student Firefighter as much as I wanted to, and as much as the crew would put up with me. Since I did not have any EMT experience on an ambulance to help with paramedic school, this was my form of EMT experience – being the fifth person on the engine and having the ability to run the EMS calls, under the guidance of the experienced crew.

For a while, I was picking up a couple of shifts a week, and working almost as much as the full-time firefighters were; I was having a lot of fun and gaining valuable experience. On a side note, I probably saw more fire and action in the 21 months I was in Oakland as a student, than I will see working in my present department. That is not meant negatively; most fire departments today do not see much fire activity. It is what it is, and I am very happy with where I am working.

In the middle of paramedic school, Greg was fortunate enough to get hired by the Stockton Fire Department, and I was fortunate enough to get hired as a paid-call Firefighter with the Elk Grove Fire Department, just south of Sacramento. It was a part-time firefighter position where we typically worked 48 hours per week, were paid about $5.00 per hour (yes, the math is correct), were not provided any medical benefits, but were able to start paying into the state retirement system, California Public Employees Retirement System (PERS). I jumped on the chance to start paying into the State retirement system.

The department was in a state of flux at the time; there were four stations that were primarily staffed with four, three-person engine companies (two that cross-staffed a truck company), and three, two person ambulances. The majority of people working in the department were like me, part-time employees without any sense of job security since the union did not represent us. That was ok to me; it was a great chance to gain experience. I had the opportunity to work 24-hour shifts, get paid, get into the retirement system, and work on an ambulance, engine or truck. What more could someone ask for, short of a full-time position?

During this time, I still had to work part-time at Longs Drugs to make ends meet, I still had the opportunity to be a Student Firefighter at Oakland, and I was still actively testing. At this point, I knew I was getting close to getting hired; it was just a matter of time. Well, as they say, when it rains, it pours. The next thing I know, I was going through two simultaneous background investigations, with the Clovis Fire Department (next to Fresno), and one with the Department I currently work for and ultimately wanted to work for.

My plan was to take the first job offer, but my heart was in the Bay Area for many reasons. I was from the Bay Area and wanted to stay in the Bay Area. I wanted to work for a larger department (something more than a few stations). I wanted the opportunity to promote and have a large number of assignments to bid for; the list goes on and on. As Murphy's Law would have it, Clovis actually offered me the job before my current Department did. It was tough, because I wanted to work in the Bay Area, but I would be stupid to turn down a job offer, especially knowing how competitive it was to become a firefighter. I graciously accepted the position in Clovis and was given a starting date.

However, my mother didn't raise a fool; I didn't want to turn down a job offer without another one guaranteed. I wasn't worried about passing my background, medical or psychological exams with the department I currently am working for, but until I received that phone call or letter providing the official job offer and notification of start date (which nowadays is no longer a guarantee as some departments have had to cancel recruit academies before the start date due to budget problems), I wasn't counting my chickens prior to them being hatched. If for some reason I didn't pass the process in the Bay Area, or for some reason they decided not to hire any of us for budget reasons or only hire a portion of the folks I was competing with, I would have found myself without any full-time firefighting job. I didn't want that to happen.

Then, go figure, a few days later, I receive a call from the Personnel Services Manager at the department I wanted to work for in the Bay Area, offering me a position. I was ecstatic – two job offers in a week or so! Now for the tough part, I had to resign from Clovis. I have really never had to resign from anything up to now, and it was tough, especially since the fire chief of Clovis, Jim Schneider, had been so personable and welcoming to me. I had heard nothing but great stuff about Clovis, and those comments were confirmed in all of my interactions with their department members.

I didn't want to burn my bridges (as you will learn, the fire service is a small, small world), and I could have taken the easy way out by calling up the fire chief or mailing them my resignation, but I felt I owed them more than that. I typed up my resignation letter (very hard to do since I consider myself a loyal person and I also felt more loyal since they were my first full-time job offer) and drove out the two and a half hours to Clovis to hand deliver it to the fire chief.

Unfortunately (or fortunately, depending on how you look at it), he wasn't in at the time, he was out of town. I met with one of the other chief officers and explained my plight. He was very respectful and understanding, and I felt extremely bad for having to do this to them, a few days before the start of my academy. At this late point, they would not be able to hire a replacement.

Two weeks later, I was starting the recruit academy in the Bay Area at the department I really wanted to work for. 18 plus years later, I am still there and enjoying every moment and extremely happy about my decision to remain in the Bay Area. I still stay in contact with a couple of the firefighters from Clovis, and I enjoy watching their department from a distance. Had I not passed my current department's hiring process for some reason, I would have still had a great position with a great department (Clovis) and would be working for a great Fire Chief, my buddy Mike Despain.

Anonymous Letter

I found the letter below at one of our fire stations, posted on the bulletin board. I don't know who posted it there, nor do I know who the author was. However, as soon as I read it, I knew it was something worth sharing with future and even current firefighters. I'm assuming this letter was intended for all firefighters, especially the newly hired firefighters, to read and understand. It has a great deal of logic and really hits home. Take the time to digest and understand what is said, and more importantly, try to put into practice the words provided here. Doing so will allow you to be the best firefighter you can be, while also allowing you to serve your community and department to the best of your ability.

Anonymous letter found in a Firehouse at the Fire Department New York (FDNY):

I, _____ having been appointed firefighter in the Fire Department of the City of New York, do solemnly swear that I will support the Constitution of the United States, and the Constitution of the State of New York, and that I will faithfully discharge the duties of a member of the Fire Department of the City of New York, according to the Laws, Regulations and Orders governing the Department, and will obey the orders and directions of my superiors, to the best of my ability. It doesn't matter how you got here. It doesn't matter how you leave here; you will leave here. It DOES matter what you do when you are here. Continue the tradition. People respect you for a reason. Do the right thing. Show the people you are a professional. Get in the books. You have the greatest job in the world, still. You are not in it for the money; support your union. It is a brotherhood, regardless of your race, gender, or nationality. You might not agree with everyone, but you will be backing them up on the line and you will be forcing a door with them. Every run could be your last so don't take them for granted because your career is going to go quick. Take the time to learn things you don't know. If you are in the truck and you're detailed to the engine for the day, take a good look at the hose bed and see which bed holds the supply line for relaying water and find out how to do it. Grab it and drag it back to the second due engine and it could save your partner's lives. If you are in the engine and you're detailed to the truck for the day take a good look at the thermal imaging camera because you have the can and might need it to get out of a sticky situation or find your officer who went down four feet away from you. That camera can save your life or his.

Know how to set up an aerial, know how to attach a pressure gauge to a standpipe and how to read it. You will never learn all there is to learn on this job. Even the top gun DAC learns something everyday. There are Department Orders filled with new procedures, glance at them at the watch instead of watching Britney Spears shave her head on the E channel.

You're going to know someone you have worked with who dies. You might not remember his name but his face is right there because you sat across from him on the back step a few times. The pain you suffer when you stand in line as the rig drives by as you hear the pipes playing entitles you to being called one of the Bravest and it is certain that the rig will drive by you. You'll meet a brother who survived and it will bring you right back to earth so quickly you won't know what hit you. The job is different than it was. We all know this. It will continue to change but one thing remains the same. When the alarm rings you will get in the rig and you may never come back. Get in knowing a little more than you did the last time you got in and this may change the outcome. Have a great St. Patrick's Day and when you walk up 5th Avenue, enjoy it because you deserve it.

Still In High School?

If you are reading this and you are still in high school, or you know someone in high school who is planning on becoming a firefighter, below are some suggested things they can be doing now before they graduate high school:

Classes to be taking:

All of the following are considered upon favorably by many fire departments, with some being considered "highly desirable:"

- Speaking and Writing:
  - Speech, journalism, leadership, communication.
- Science:
  - Physics, chemistry, biology.
- Computer Skills:
  - Basic usage, Microsoft Office product usage (Word, Excel, PowerPoint).
- Physical Fitness:
  - Scholastic sports, weigh training, gym classes.
- Mechanical:
  - Wood shop, auto shop, metal shop.
- Math:
  - Algebra, geometry.
- English:

- ○ Reading, writing.
- Foreign language:
  - ○ Any foreign language.
- General:
  - ○ Cooking, CPR, first aid.

General experience to obtain:

All of the following are considered favorably by many fire departments, with some being considered "highly desirable:"

- Volunteering in any capacity:
  - ○ Make sure you keep track of your hours on your resume.
- Mechanical ability / construction trades experience.
- Teaching experience.
- Household maintenance:
  - ○ Cleaning, general repairs.
- Communication skills:
  - ○ Written, oral, interpersonal.

General suggestions to assist you in a fire service career:

- Make sure you actually graduate high school with a diploma, and don't settle for a G.E.D. or equivalent.
- Start visiting fire stations to get an idea of what the career is about, and to start networking with current firefighters.
- Start researching the fire service, starting with your local department and then working outwards to start to see how one department differs from another (ranks, organizational structure, what they call their apparatus, what their apparatus look like, what they each have to offer, etc.).
- Subscribe to free fire service related email lists:
  - ○ **Daily Dispatch** – http://www.dailydispatch.com
  - ○ **Fire Engineering Magazine** – http://www.fireengineering.com

- ○ **Firehouse Magazine** – http://www.firehouse.com
  - ○ **Fire Rescue Magazine** – http://www.firefighternation.com
  - ○ **Firefighter Close Calls** – http://www.firefighterclosecalls.com
- Plan on attending a 2-year college to obtain your EMT certification, Firefighter 1 Academy certification, and a 2-year degree in Fire Technology.
- Keep your driving record clean, free of tickets and accidents:
  - ○ Something that many candidates get disqualified for during the background investigation.
- Keep your criminal record clean, free of arrests or convictions:
  - ○ Something that many candidates get disqualified for during the background investigation.
- Pick your friends wisely:
  - ○ Something that many candidates get disqualified for during the background investigation.
- Don't use drugs. Period.
- Don't drink alcohol. Period.
- Don't smoke. Period.
- Don't get a tattoo visible when in a t-shirt and shorts:
  - ○ While it may be the cool thing to do, many departments will not hire people with visible tattoos. Plus you'll probably regret it in your later years.
  - ○ Save the money, use it instead for helping yourself become a firefighter.
- Basically – STAY OUT OF TROUBLE, DON'T DO STUPID STUFF YOU'LL REGRET AND DON'T HANG OUT WITH THE WRONG CROWD!

You may be wondering about many of the above items...is the fire service looking for perfect people? No. We realize nobody is perfect. People make mistakes, but hopefully not the same mistake twice and hopefully not a serious mistake that you don't get a second chance to recover from. We're looking for individuals with positive character traits that begin at a young age (honesty, integrity, ethics, teamwork, responsible, mature, leader, personable, social, charismatic, just to name a few).

Why Do You Want To Be A Firefighter?

Why do you want to be a firefighter? You need to ask yourself that, and you also need to find out, what does a firefighter really do? If you think fight fires and save lives 24 hours a day, 7 days a week, 365 days a year, you're in for a surprise!

Now brace yourself: The average firefighter will probably never "grab someone from the clutches of death" and make that career lifesaving rescue that many read about or hear about. The average firefighter may go months without seeing any fire in person while on duty and performing legal activities (sorry, had to say that; by the way, there is a serious arson problem among fire service members around the country who have either been bored or frustrated by not seeing enough fire – so they decide to create their own).

About eighty percent of the call volume for most fire departments is related to Emergency Medical Service (EMS) responses, which include vehicle accidents. Fire responses typically only make up about five percent or less of the call volume for most fire departments, and actual fires are much lower than that number. So, if you're getting into this career to fight fire and save lives, you will probably be disappointed because you probably won't be doing much of either. But if you're getting into the career to help people, serve your community, and make a positive difference, this may be the career for you. Please don't use those reasons for becoming a firefighter when you get to your oral interview.

Before what I've said discourages you, realize that I am saying that to enlighten you, not discourage you. I have seen many firefighters get hired and then find out we don't fight fire every day and that they will be lucky if they ever "rescue" someone. Now don't get me wrong, I think there are numerous things we do and can do to help reduce the loss of life and reduce the injuries from fires, emergencies and disasters, through fire prevention, community education, and disaster preparedness, however it is really hard to put a finger on whether what we did prevention and education wise actually worked. It doesn't mean we should stop trying – if anything we should try do more of those items, only because when the next "big one" hits, no single fire department will have the sufficient resources and personnel to do everything a community expects of them.

Most fire departments don't even have sufficient resources and personnel to handle more than one significant event, let alone simultaneous events. Chances are in our careers, staffing levels will not be increasing (we will be lucky to maintain what we currently have); due to a variety of reasons – some of which are within our control, some that are not. Governmental agencies around the Country are faced with declining revenues and ever-increasing personnel related costs such as healthcare and retirement benefits and fuel costs, not to mention costs in general to run an operation such as a fire department.

Because of this, the fire service will need to continue to be creative at doing less with less or different with less (sorry, I hate the term doing more with less because I don't think it is possible) or determining how to be a part of the solution – not the problem, to continue to survive in the world as we know it.

What Does A Firefighter Do?

What does a firefighter do? Fight fire? Save lives and property? Protect the environment? Help people? Yes to all of the above, and much, much more.

A few years ago, while I was working as the Fire Technology Coordinator at Chabot College (I still work there on a part-time basis as an instructor), I had the opportunity to evaluate a few of our instructors (each instructor receives regular evaluations). One of the requirements of the evaluation process is to have the students complete an instructor evaluation and provide us with feedback on the instructor's performance. Two of the classes come to mind, one being the wildland firefighting class and the other being the fire prevention technology class. After sitting down and reading all of the completed instructor evaluations, it became very clear to me that many of the students do not have a clue as to what they are getting into or what the job of a firefighter consists of.

Let me take the wildland firefighting class. This class is meant to be an introduction to basic (not advanced) wildland firefighting, and is required by the State Fire Marshal's Office as part of the State Firefighter 1 educational requirements. Some of the comments I received were:

- *"A lot of information that I will probably never use, but I guess it is important."*
- *"Great class if I wanted to work for the California Department of Forestry (CDF is now known as Cal Fire – a state fire agency that primarily deals with wildland fire suppression and prevention)."*

- *"I guess if I were going to be a wildland firefighter, this would be good information. Since I want to work for a city fire department, this information probably won't be helpful."*

Ok, let me "burst the bubble" and explain something to you up front. I don't know of too many locations in the United States that do not have the potential for wildland fires to occur. For these students that live in California and plan to work in California, they are really misinformed if they think that getting hired by a city fire department will allow them to not have to deal with wildland fires.

There is a city in the San Francisco Bay Area that is surrounded by water, the city of Alameda. While those firefighters do not have any land that would be considered wildland urban interface, as would many of the Bay Area cities that border the hills that circle the Bay Area, they do have something in common.

Being a California Fire Department means that they are part of the California State Mutual Aid System, and may be mobilized at any time to fight a wildland fire in any part of the state. For those that say "I didn't sign up to fight wildland fires," think again. When you took the oath of office as a firefighter in the State of California, you agreed to be part of the mutual aid system. Oh yes, Alameda is next to Oakland, a city that had a major conflagration (massive fire) in 1991.

Virtually every San Francisco Bay Area Fire Department as well as most fire departments within a few hundred-mile radius offered up engines to assist with the fire fight. So, while your jurisdiction might not have wildland urban interface area to protect (and that is even rare, at least in California), I bet your neighboring departments do and will be asking you to assist if the fire gets big enough.

The point here is that a firefighter of today is considered to be "all risk." Meaning you have to be trained in virtually every type of scenario possible, not just structure firefighting. We're doing EMS, we're doing Weapons of Mass Destruction, we're doing rescue, we're doing hazardous materials and oh yes, we're doing wildland firefighting. I used to think one of the only places in the U.S. that a firefighter wouldn't have to worry about wildland firefighting would be in New

York, working for the Fire Department of New York. Well, think again; have you ever been to Staten Island, one of the five boroughs?

The FDNY actually has a few brush firefighting trucks stationed on Staten Island. When I got hired, I remember hearing from a chief that is now retired "we're not a wildland fire department." The sad thing is that I still hear comments like that from people around the United States, and especially from California. Keep thinking that way and you're likely to get someone injured or killed because of not being completely prepared for the situations you may be presented with.

Now, let me take the fire prevention technology class. This class is also meant to be an introductory class that exposes the student to basic (not advanced) fire prevention practices. Some of the comments I received in the instructor evaluations were:

- *"I want to be an engine firefighter, not a fire inspector. Not sure why I have to have this class to be a firefighter."*
- *"Too much knowledge for a firefighter to have."*
- *"I'm only taking this class because I want the degree to become a firefighter."*

As a firefighter, you are going to be tasked with doing commercial (fire prevention) inspections in many jurisdictions. Most departments do not have the luxury of having a large staff of fire prevention inspectors, especially to do only fire prevention activities. In many departments, due to budget reductions, the fire prevention bureau is the first to go. This requires the engine companies at the stations to pick up the load. Besides getting the chance to get the companies out to meet their customers, performing fire prevention inspections also allows us to perform public education and pre-plan our first-due areas so that we are prepared when "the big one hits."

I'd rather be familiar with a building that is not on fire so that when it is on fire, I have an idea of what is inside and what type of hazards or situations we may be presented with. In addition to wildland firefighting and fire prevention inspections, what else does a firefighter do? I think the question should be what does a firefighter not do? Have you ever heard the phrase, "jack of all trades, master of none?" That is the job of a firefighter in a nutshell.

In no specific order of priority or frequency, here are some of the things firefighters do either on an everyday or occasional basis:

- Emergency Medical Service (EMS) calls.
- Invalid assist (also known as service) calls (help assist someone back into bed or their chair because they are unable to do so themselves, or with the help of others that care for them).
- Vehicle fires.
- Structure fires.
- Wildland fires.
- Trash / dumpster fires.
- Fire alarm sounding calls (residential and commercial buildings).
- Smoke investigation calls (inside and outside the building).
- Gas investigation calls (inside and outside the building).
- Hazardous materials calls.
- Public service calls (the catchall call, anything that will assist the public).
- Vehicle accidents.
- Rescue calls.
- Assist with removing animals in danger or potentially being a danger to others.
- Assist people with directions (people know that the fire department has maps, so all types of people ask us for directions, including delivery drivers and people from out of town).
- Provide fire station tours.
- Visit schools to do public education demonstrations, show the fire apparatus to the students, talk about careers in the fire service.
- Teach the public CPR.
- Teach the public how to use fire extinguishers.
- Test / maintain fire hydrants.
- Maintain accurate records and reports.
- Document patient care as an EMT or paramedic.

- Maintain the fire station / department facilities, including:
    - Yard maintenance.
    - Cleaning the bathrooms, kitchen, day room, etc.
    - Changing light bulbs, painting as needed, washing windows, etc.
- Maintain fire apparatus, including:
    - Checking and maintaining fluid levels.
    - Performing routine maintenance.
    - Washing, waxing and detailing.
- Maintain tools and equipment, including:
    - Keeping them free from rust and wear.
    - Keeping them oiled and painted as appropriate.
- Perform weed abatement inspections.
- Provide fire investigative services.
- Provide social services / basic counseling to assist the public in times of grieving or distress. This could be from the result of family or friends that have died or have been severely injured, or from people that are just not having a good day or life.
- Assist people with basic plumbing, basic electrical, basic construction, basic mechanical and any other basic need you can think of.
- Why do people call us at 3 in the morning, versus calling a plumber when their water heater breaks?
    - They know we will come when they call 911.
    - They don't know whom else to call.
    - They know we will help them out.
    - They don't want to spend the money to hire a professional.
- The list goes on and on.....

Before you make the commitment to put countless hours of preparation, energy, and effort into becoming a firefighter, I sure hope you realize what you are getting yourself into. Well, if you are this far along in the process (which I assume you are since you are reading this), you may still learn a few things you did not previously know were things a firefighter actually does in the course of a day.

What a firefighter does in one fire department may slightly (or drastically) differ from what a firefighter does in another fire department in the nearby vicinity or across the country. Watch television shows and it is not uncommon to see firefighters sitting around the kitchen table, joking and having fun, and maybe even watching television or sleeping, during the day time.

Rarely do you see firefighters portrayed as doing "busy work," or actually doing productive work such as actual pre-fire planning (and that does not mean going shopping for the daily necessary fire station meal; it means actually walking through existing occupancies or buildings under construction to learn how they are constructed and analyze how they would mitigate an emergency), doing company fire prevention inspections, creating and updating pre-fire plans, training, performing physical fitness, or just maintaining their fire station, apparatus and/or tools and equipment.

So, if you watch a television show, news story, or even a movie relating or depicting firefighters, how do you usually see us portrayed? In my experience, one of two ways: we are either on the job at a working incident of some form or fashion, or we are back at the station either preparing a meal or killing time waiting to get toned out for the next run. I'm not saying this is bad, as much as I'm saying it is an unrealistic portrayal of what a firefighter does in many (not all) departments. In some departments, that is the routine; go on a call or wait for the next call to come. Yes, there may be a little housework completed, and a rig check out here or there, but is the crew spending a couple of hours a day training, and doing what it takes to be the best they can be? I'll let you make that call.

However, getting back to what a firefighter really does, I think it would open a lot of people's eyes – including the eyes of future firefighters, if they realized that a firefighter may do more things than just run calls and sit around the kitchen table waiting for the next run. I find it amazing when fire departments hire firefighters, who suddenly hate running medical calls, or hate going out on Band-Aid calls, or hate doing public education details or company inspections, or whatever.

We have all heard some form of complaint (after someone got

off probation of course), where a firefighter is not fond of doing a certain task, or even worse, pleads ignorant or states "I didn't sign up to _____," or "that is not in my job description." As great of a career we have, I still hear things like that (luckily rarely in my great department), but more commonly when I talk to others around the country or read about the actions or statements a certain firefighter may provide.

I remember hearing one of my former Emergency Medical Technician (EMT) students who had been working at a big city fire department for a few years, complain about having to go on the "B.S. medical calls." I remember when he was in EMT training, he loved the medical calls and he couldn't wait to be a firefighter to help people and make their day better. I asked him, "What happened to the passion and fire you used to have? You now sound like a crusty old salt that has been on the job for 30 years and burned out!" He actually thought about it and said that he was so used to hearing the other firefighters on the job complain about the medical calls that he must have naturally started talking like them. I was blown away. It was a good reality check for him, and it was a reality check for me too: sometimes we eat our young and can be our own worst enemy.

The lesson learned for you as a future firefighter – do not let this happen to you at all costs! Always remember the passion and desire you had before you were hired. That passion and desire to be a firefighter when you were in the oral interview telling your prospective employer how much you wanted to help others, how much you wanted to be the best firefighter you could be and how much of an asset you were going to be to that community if they took the chance at hiring you.

Before any future firefighter determines this is the career for them, I hope they realize they may be called upon on any given shift, to do a number of different things, and even possess the necessary knowledge, skills, and abilities to accomplish the following things at some point during their fire department career, depending on the department they end up working for. Note: some of these things the department will formally teach you how to accomplish. However, many of these things the department will expect you to bring with you in the form of life experience or learn on-the-job from other firefighters.

Here is the job description from the position of firefighter from a California Fire Department that could be for any fire department across the country:

Position of Firefighter:

To respond to fire alarms, medical emergency, and other emergency activities in the protection of life and property; and to participate in fire prevention, training and station and equipment maintenance activities.

Essential Job Functions:

- Respond to fire alarms with assigned company.
- Lay and connect hose lines.
- Hold nozzles and direct water streams.
- Raise and climb ladders.
- Provide basic life support during medical incidents, assessing and initiating patient care until relieved by proper medical personnel.
- Operate all types of portable fire extinguishers, hand tools, power tools and appliances, salvage covers, forcible entry tools, emergency medical equipment and other rescue equipment.
- Participate in fire drills.
- Serve as instructor as assigned.
- Attends training sessions.
- Maintain regular and consistent attendance.
- Promote and maintain safety in the workplace.
- Work cooperatively with others.
- Shut down natural gas and electrical services to structures.
- Respond to hazardous materials incidents.
- Participate in the Fire Prevention Program providing various public relations services, including facility tours (fire station tours), public education seminars and other public events.

- Respond to inquiries from the public.
- Assist in investigating fire origin and cause.
- May be requested to respond to fire calls during non-duty hours.
- Control traffic.
- Participate as a member of the County Haz Mat team.
- Inventory supplies.
- Maintain records.
- Can serve as "acting positions" when certified.
- Clean station quarters and equipment and maintain a clean and orderly condition in and about the firehouse.
- Perform minor building maintenance.
- Operate radio-telephone equipment.
- Assist in overhaul and salvage operations.
- Test and maintain fire hoses and hydrants.
- Perform related duties as assigned.

NOTE: Remember that last one – "perform related duties as assigned." So, when you complain to your captain or chief "why do I have to do that," or "that is not in my job description," remember that catch all phrase that is listed in most job descriptions – "perform related duties as required."

Additionally, here are some "essential firefighting functions" from a big city fire department in the Midwest so you can compare what a firefighter in California may do in the job description above to what a firefighter may do in another part of the United States:

Essential Firefighting Functions:

Physical Task Statements:

- Put on and wear protective equipment.
- Open hydrant to charge the hose.
- Use 1 ¾" hose as an attack line.
- Use equipment (e.g., ax, sledge hammer, etc.) to make forcible entries.

- Enter smoke filled buildings/rooms with a hose in hand while wearing full protective clothing.
- Crawl on a floor and if you cannot see, feel for the heat of the fire source.
- Systematically search for trapped persons.
- Drag victims with the help of another firefighter.
- Screw the hose connection to the hydrant.
- Drag charged 1 ¾" hose up stairs and around furniture when fighting fire.
- Carry victims with the help of another firefighter.
- Use a hose clamp to clamp a charged/uncharged hose.
- Wrap a hose around a hydrant to stretch it out and ensure it reaches the plug.
- Climb stairs wearing full equipment while responding to a call for service.
- Carry heavy equipment (hose pack, medical box, air bottles), up stairs while wearing full equipment.
- Support a ladder, and raise the halyard to extend to the desired length, and then lower into objective.
- Climb an aerial ladder wearing full equipment.
- Hold an 1 ¾" hose unassisted and open the nozzle.
- Drag a victim out of a building unassisted while wearing full turnout gear.
- Drag accordion folded or flat load, uncharged 2 ½" or 3" hose until it is fully extended.
- Drag charged 1 ¾" hose unassisted.
- Reload hose and put it back on the engine/quint.
- Remove heavy equipment (i.e., smoke ejector, positive pressure fan, medical box) from the apparatus; transport and place it in operation unassisted.
- Use a pike pole to pull down a ceiling.
- Carry a victim out of a building unassisted while wearing full turnout gear.
- Carry people unassisted down ladders while wearing full turnout gear.

- Carry people unassisted via stairs wearing full turnout gear.
- Carry a section of rolled hose unassisted.
- Lower ladders and re-bed them onto the truck/quint.
- Remove an extension ladder from the apparatus unassisted and carry it to its destination.
- Operate a charged line from confined spaces.
- Operate foam equipment.
- Operate a line from heights (e.g. rooftops).
- While on a ladder, direct water at fire.
- Operate the ladder pipe from an aerial platform.
- Extend the booster line to a fire.
- Hoist equipment to upper levels by a rope.

Mechanical Tasks:

- Make and unmake coupling connections.
- Operate power tools (e.g., chain saw, circular saw, etc.) during the course of firefighting activities.
- Remove the hydrant cap with a wrench.
- Safely shut off utility services to buildings in emergency situations.
- Operate heavy equipment (e.g., "jaws-of-life," etc.) in response to an emergency.
- Operate electrical/gas shut-off valves.
- Set up aerial ladder jacks, place chocks, and then position and raise ladder.
- Make openings for ventilation using equipment (e.g., saws, axes, etc.).
- Drive firefighting/emergency equipment to and from a scene.
- Respond to hazards related to electrical emergencies.
- Operate a fire extinguisher.
- Inspect a pumper during operation; check gauges.

Rescue & Fire Suppression:

- Be aware of electrical lines when setting up ladders and directing water streams.
- Seek the source of a fire and extinguish.
- Determine the safest evacuation route.
- Evacuate persons from a fire area.
- Assist at a water rescue.
- Determine the stability of supporting surfaces.
- Assist at a water rescue.
- Calculate friction loss in hose to ensure the proper water pressure is provided to successfully put out a fire.
- Calculate, achieve, and maintain correct water pressure for hose lines.
- Determine when to open up roofs, walls and doors.
- Calculate the height of a building in feet from its floors to ensure ladders are elevated to the proper height.
- Determine the number of lines to hook up to successfully put out a fire.
- Select the proper number of hoses required to reach the fire.
- Determine the correct stream to use.
- Calculate gallons per minute out of a particular size hose.
- Calculate the height of a building in feet from its floors to ensure the proper number of hoses are selected to reach the fire.
- Recommend assistance from law enforcement, medical, coroner, or utility personnel as needed.

Administrative:

- Write descriptions of situations in medical reports.
- Complete incident reports on the computer.
- Write building fire inspection reports.

Emergency Medical Service:

- Use the necessary tools to free trapped persons.
- Perform CPR or other appropriate cardiac emergency procedures.
- Rescue victims and apply resuscitation measures as necessary.
- Administer oxygen to victims.
- Extricate people from automobiles.
- Remove persons from entrapments; safely free victims.
- Prepare and transfer a patient to an emergency vehicle.
- Treat shock.
- Control the bleeding of a patient.
- Identify and respond to hazards at the scene.
- Gather patient medical history information from a patient or family.
- Provide concise and complete information to paramedics about patient status.
- Prepare the emergency vehicle for the next response, including decontaminating and disinfecting unit and equipment, restocking supplies, inspecting equipment, and making or arranging for necessary repairs or replacement.
- Control the emergency scene to protect yourself, coworkers, and the patient.
- Set up and operate the Automatic External Defibrillator.
- Immobilize fractures.
- Assist in childbirth.
- Assess the emergency scene and request assistance if necessary.
- Accurately take incoming calls or information from the dispatcher regarding requests for emergency medical services.
- Control a hysterical patient requiring medical attention.
- Bandage wounds.
- Administer glucose to diabetics.
- Comfort family, friends, and bystanders at a fire scene or medical facility.
- Calm mentally disturbed patient to ensure they can be cared for successfully.

- Monitor and provide needed care when transporting a patient to a medical facility.

Hazardous Materials (Haz Mat):

- Respond to the release or potential release of hazardous materials.
- Utilize and maintain personal/chemical protective equipment.
- Complete required hazardous materials training.
- Read haz mat reference materials at a scene to provide the proper response to a hazardous materials spill.
- Perform defensive mitigation techniques (e.g., diking, damming, diverting, etc.).
- Apply a foam blanket.
- Spray chemicals on a fire.
- Perform offensive mitigation techniques (e.g., plugging, patching, etc.).

Fire Prevention/Inspections:

- Inspect commercial buildings for fire hazards defined in fire codes and state law (e.g., building interiors/exteriors, hazardous materials storage, and inspection of standpipes, smoke detectors, fire extinguishers, fire alarms, and sprinkler systems.
- Determine fire code violations.
- Accurately document fire code violations.
- Inspect residential complexes of three or more families for fire hazards.
- Seek compliance with fire codes by a building owner.
- Note tactical information such as location of exists to assist in future operations.
- Investigate complaints of fire hazards, dangers, or violations.

Training/Drills:

- Maintain physical fitness standards of the department.

- Learn how to successfully attack a fire.
- Participate in on-going training drills to develop and maintain proficiency.
- Learn about extricating victims from vehicles.
- Learn about forcible entry into buildings.
- Read and comprehend written training materials.
- Learn the most direct routes to various addresses in a response area.
- Learn about ventilation methods to aid in extinguishing a fire.
- Learn about the characteristics of and proper uses of ladders.
- Learn fire department rules and regulations.
- Learn, practice and perform evolutions.
- Learn about various methods of rescue.
- Learn the locations of streets, water mains and hydrants in a response area.
- Learn about building construction to determine how a fire might react in that building, and to ensure the safety of those working in and around the building.
- Learn about hydraulics and pump operations.
- Learn about fire behavior. Learn about ropes and knots to accomplish rescues.
- Learn about appropriate fire streams given factors that can affect the flow of water through the air.
- Learn about caring for hoses, hose lays and hose use.
- Learn about various causes of fire.
- Learn about water supply systems.
- Learn about salvage and overhaul.
- Learn about ropes and knots to stabilize vehicles.
- Learn about ropes and knots to successfully haul tools.
- Learn about fire alarms and automatic sprinkler systems.

Fire Station Duties:

- Report for duty on time.
- Maintain positive working relationships with crewmembers.

- Present a clean and neat appearance.
- Maintain a clean and neat working and living environment at the fire station.
- Answer routine phone calls in the station.
- Maintain the exterior of fire station; lawns, walkways, and driveways.
- Store fire equipment and supplies.
- Make your own bed and change linens when appropriate.
- Plan and cook meals.

Fire Investigations/Post-Fire Duties:

- Inspect, service, and perform tests of all SCBA to ensure they are working properly.
- Maintain all personal protective equipment.
- Keep all tools and equipment in working order.
- Maintain an inventory of tools and equipment.
- Replenish supplies when needed.
- After a fire is extinguished, check for smoldering fire inside walls and ceiling.
- Perform regular service tests on all apparatus.
- Search for missing people.
- Preserve evidence at fire scene.
- Perform overhaul operations.
- Inspect, clean, and polish equipment and apparatus by hand.
- Fill pressurized water extinguisher.
- Secure accident/fire scene.
- Remove burned and charred waste.
- Put furniture in one location and protect it with salvage covers.
- Remove hoses from drying racks and store them.
- Remove all used equipment from rigs after a fire for cleaning.

Communication:

- Listen to the dispatcher, other fire vehicles, and commanding officers by radio to determine course of action.
- Exchange necessary information with other firefighters at a scene.
- Advise the commanding officer of fire conditions, hazards, and exposures at the scene.
- Talk with other firefighters at an emergency scene to determine the best courses of action.
- Communicate with the superior officers during a fire.
- Clearly and accurately communicate patient information / care to medical staff.

Environmental/Working Conditions:

- Avoid and protect against infectious agents.
- Avoid and protect against hazardous substances through inhalation, injection, ingestion, and absorption.
- Protect against possible burn injuries.
- Fight fires in smoky buildings when visibility is nonexistent.
- Work quickly to suppress a fire.
- Fight fires in smoky buildings when visibility is poor.
- Fight fires in extremely hot environments.
- Perform on ladders.
- Prevent exposure to sharp objects.
- Protect against uninstalled or unshielded electrical equipment.
- Perform in wet, muddy, icy, and/or slippery areas.
- Prevent exposures to noxious odors.
- Work in confined spaces in cramped body positions.
- Perform physically demanding tasks under extreme fluctuations in temperature.
- Fight fires in sub zero temperatures.
- Withstand strong vibrations (e.g., riding in emergency vehicles or operating power tools).

- Work on or around moving machinery or equipment.
- Perform wearing full equipment.
- Work 24-hour shifts with little or no sleep.
- Protect against smoke and dust.
- Protect against radiation hazards.
- Avoid and protect against high noise levels when riding in emergency vehicles.

Knowledge areas:

- EMS Knowledge. Knowledge of first aid procedures; knowledge of CPR; knowledge of blood borne pathogens; knowledge of medical protocol.
- Mechanical Comprehension. Knowledge of various tools and their use; knowledge of mechanical concepts (how engines operate, basic hydraulics, and other related concepts).
- Emergency Procedure Knowledge. Knowledge of procedures for emergencies and unusual events; knowledge of radio codes and procedures.
- Building Construction. Knowledge of the materials and construction features of buildings (e.g., doors, windows, walls, and locks); knowledge of building construction.
- Use of Language. Knowledge of the correct spelling of words; knowledge of grammar rules; knowledge of punctuation rules.
- Knowledge of vehicle extrication techniques.
- Knowledge of fire department rules, regulations, and policies.
- Knowledge of hazardous materials.
- Knowledge of fire behavior.
- Knowledge of street layouts and the location of hydrants and water mains in a response area.
- Knowledge of fire codes and regulations to ensure proper inspection.
- Ability to understand and interpret basic chemical, biological, and radiological terms and data.

Public Relations:

- Use tact and diplomacy in dealing with the public.
- Interact and work with citizens.
- Provide fire education programs to the public when requested.
- Make public education calls.
- Refer people to agencies that provide social services.
- Conduct fire station tours when requested and approved.

Have you figured it out by now, that a
firefighter is <u>not</u> just a firefighter!

Looking at all of those above duties of a firefighter, it suffices to say that to be a great firefighter, you would have to be skilled in a number of different trades. One of my fire technology instructors (can't remember who) told me a firefighter needs to know about 26 different trades and careers, in order to be a good firefighter. I actually did the math and it's higher than 26. At first, that sounded unrealistic, but when you think about it, it is highly possible a firefighter can be called upon at a moment's notice to do any of the following trades, professions, jobs, or careers as part of their daily routine on duty (and I don't mean as part of a side job off-duty) whether at the fire station or on a response.

Below are the typical roles a firefighter could find themselves filling on any given shift:

1. Plumber
2. Electrician
3. Carpenter
4. Social worker
5. Psychologist
6. Psychiatrist
7. Auto detailer
8. Auto repair person
9. Maid
10. Mechanic

11. Teacher

12. Chef/Cook

13. Administrative Assistant (Secretary)

14. Dishwasher

15. Janitor/Custodian

16. Landscaper

17. Painter

18. Police officer

19. Service station attendant

20. Accountant

21. Financial advisor

22. Truck driver

23. Facilities manager

24. Food server

25. Waiter/waitress

26. Recreational coordinator

27. Career planner/advisor

28. Maintenance person (handyman)

29. Dietician

30. Appliance repairperson

31. Heating, Ventilation, Air Conditioning (HVAC) repairperson

32. Tow truck driver

33. Customer service representative

34. Public educator

35. Public information provider

36. Computer technician

37. Television repair person / troubleshooter

38. Fire prevention inspector

39. Fire investigator

40. Medical professional (first responder, EMT, paramedic)

41. Hazardous materials first responder

42. Rescue technician (basic or advanced)

43. Firefighter (oh, yes, on occasion, we are still asked to put out fires!)

See what I mean, jack-of-all-trades, and master of none? I don't know of any other trades that require a person to have so much knowledge in so many different areas to be successful. The job of a firefighter today is definitely not the same as it was 30 years ago, and will probably not be the same 30 years from now. Many fire departments did not respond to any EMS calls 30 years ago, and those that did, did not have EMS calls making up 70 to 80% of their annual call volume.

Face it, fires in general are on the decline and I don't really see those numbers spiking upward anywhere in the near future. These are reasons why you see firefighters doing so many different things to please their customers and why we are typically doing less with less or different with less.

I have probably missed a few professions or trades, so feel free to add your own to the list to educate others about what a firefighter really does. Take a deep look at what a firefighter does from the time they arrive at the firehouse to the time they leave the firehouse. Whether or not they respond to a single call, they may still do many of the above items while on duty at the firehouse. Talk to most senior firefighters, and I bet they can provide examples of having to do a good majority (if not more) of those abovementioned items at some point in their career, obviously some more than others.

Some people forget that we are the ones people call when they cannot figure out what to do, or more commonly, cannot afford to call a repair person for, especially at three o'clock in the morning, on a holiday. While they may not want to pay triple time for a plumber to come to their house to stop the water flowing from a burst pipe, they have no problem calling 9-1-1 knowing we will come and at least stop the problem, with some thinking we may solve the problem. If nothing else, we will probably stop the immediate problem, and then direct them to who they need to contact to fully solve the problem.

If you haven't figured it out by now, I hope you do very quickly realize we don't just "save lives and property anymore," and that we are really jacks-of-all-trades. I won't go as far as adding "but masters of none," because I hope if nothing else, we are masters at our profession and the core expectations of what we are here for: serving our community and making a positive difference every day we are on duty.

Whether you agree with it or not, the bottom line is that we are going to be doing more to please the public and keep our jobs; not doing so will only lead to our slow demise or at least diminish the levels of service we're providing today (and trust me, I don't know of any department nationwide that can honestly say they are staffed the way they should be, and have more firefighters, fire stations, and fire apparatus than they need). What you'll see is that most departments nationwide are at the same (or less) staffing levels they were at 20 or more years ago, but that their call volume has increased tremendously in that time, and their department has not kept up with the growth.

If you do not embrace the challenges a firefighter faces every day (and I don't mean life-threatening or life-saving challenges, those are usually far and few), you will be frustrated and unhappy. Instead of getting angry with the folks who call 9-1-1 for our assistance, do your best to have patience, tolerance, and most of all empathy and compassion for their current situation.

To you, it may be a B.S. call; to them, it may be the emergency of a lifetime. More importantly though, we need to educate our future firefighters and let them know we don't just save lives and property (less than 5% of our job in most departments) and that instead, we are here to help the people who pay our salaries by solving the problems they are faced with in a courteous and professional way, to ensure we leave the impression that they cannot live without us!

Lessons Learned From Past Students

Before we get any deeper, I wanted to share a couple of emails received from past students that wanted to share some nuggets with other future firefighters, based on their lessons learned:

From Jon:

Maybe there should be a Fire Service Technology 40 Class (note – there is currently no such class, this would be a new class that is the first class a student takes at the college) – Reality of the Fire Service. This class suggestion should be one of the first classes that new students should attend. This would have them do a study/paper on the reality of the fire service. Have them talk to firefighters, do research on call volume, what types of calls, and how many fire calls vs. medical calls the department of their choice responds to. Hopefully this will weed out the fire hungry folks that think the California Fire Service is like the FDNY or other older cities that still run fire calls almost (if not always) daily. Just a suggestion. I completed my test with LA City Fire today. There were 40 math questions and 40 reading comprehension questions. So study up on your math! Take care.

From Brian:

I ended up staying last night. I was the one in the front row at your firefighter preparation seminar (the one answering questions all night). You are a wealth of knowledge, but some of my classmates whine that you don't sound too optimistic or encouraging about the fire service. The way I look at it is that you are just trying to paint a realistic picture of the fire service as you have experience in the last decade. If the information you give out depresses or discourages anybody, then I say GOOD! Just a few less people to deal with who are not serious about the process of earning their badge. I appreciate all your advice this semester as I have re-entered my training to become a firefighter. I feel that the extra life years have given me a good advantage and the right mental attitude and maturity to go after this career with everything I have. I'm going to drop off applications in Oakdale and Fresno today and was just in Phoenix testing last week. Phoenix was my first test and man was that an eye opener. About 3000 people there on test day!

From David:

This one comes from a student who I had to give an "F" to after he failed the final exam by two points. The passing score on the final written exam, which consisted of 100 multiple-choice questions, was 80%. All he had to do was get 80 out of 100 questions correct. He only got 78 questions correct, and we do not allow make-ups or second chances. He had all semester to be successful, and while we don't spoon-feed students, we do provide lots of information for them to be successful.

Here was the email I received from David:

So really all I needed was to get TWO more questions right on that test and I would be home free? Are you sure there is no possible way of me passing? I really worked my butt off. I did every extra credit homework and assignment, and even went to the two Saturday classes. This just does not seem right at all!

My commentary for you to learn from:

- When you test for your dream fire department, do you think they're going to give you a "break"? No! If passing is 80, or

70, or whatever, you need to at least score the minimum to continue. Allowing someone to continue who doesn't meet the minimum helps nobody. Do you want the paramedic treating YOUR chest pain that missed the passing mark on their final exam by two points, but was allowed to pass because someone felt it was appropriate to lower the standard for this person?

- We don't want you passing a class based on extra credit. You need to pass any class based on the core competencies – written examinations and skills examinations. The extra credit should only be there to maybe allow you to go from a C to a B, or a B to an A.

- Even if he only missed by ONE question, I wouldn't have any more sympathy than I do now, which is none. I tell students on day one that just squeaking by does not cut it. I say that because this class the person failed was the Introduction to Fire Protection Organization – basically the first Fire Science class at the college. If they can't pass this class with a high B or more importantly an A, how are they going to be when the heat really gets turned on when they get into EMT, Firefighter 1 Academy, or even Paramedic training – all of which are extremely difficult. I honestly thought Paramedic training was tougher than obtaining my Bachelor's Degree.

- Just because he supposedly worked his butt off, does that mean he gets to pass? Did his parents and our society fail him because we give trophies out for just trying? Yes and yes. Many people work their butt off (or so they think), but study the wrong things or do not have good study habits.

- Regarding "this just does not seem right at all," oh well – nobody said life would be fair or right, did they?

From Jerran:

This one comes from a student who wanted to share his good news and reinforce some of the key points we try to instill in students.

Here was the email I received from Jerran:

Just wanted to let you know that they posted the results of the written test for Sac Metro and I passed! We go for the CPAT orientation on the weekend of the 23rd and 24th. It was interesting how the directions they gave for the orientation really meshed with what you spoke about this morning at class about following directions. The orientation seems to have two equally important purposes. First familiarizing yourself with the equipment used and the events and second, which seemed equally important, following directions, wearing proper clothing, showing up 10 minutes early to your scheduled time, etc. Anyway just wanted to pass on the great news, have a great week. Thanks!

My commentary for you to learn from:

- He hit the nail on the head – following directions is paramount to your success, as is showing up early and taking the time to familiarize yourself with the events you're asked to complete.
- Listen to the key points shared by your instructors, parents, adults, etc. I know when we're younger (like I was), we tend to blow off some of what our instructors, parents, adults, etc. say because we're young or for whatever reason. Been there, done that, got the t-shirt. But, it's funny as I get older I realize most of the advice they offered was true. Had I just listened to them earlier, maybe I would have learned from some of their mistakes!

From Chris:

This one comes from a student who was extremely frustrated that he had not yet been hired in the city he lives in (and I guess felt he was entitled to be hired in). He got so frustrated he asked me my opinion about a letter he was going to write to the Fire Chief to try to have her change the City's hiring practices to get him hired:

Here was the email I received from Chris:

Dear Chief Joanne Hayes-White:

I am writing to you in regards to the hiring process for the position of H-2 Firefighter. As a San Francisco native and an aspiring Firefighter, I am suggesting a proposal to our department. Instead of spending excessive time and money on hiring I am suggesting that a residency requirement be imposed. San Francisco wouldn't be the first department to do such a thing. Surprisingly some of the top fire departments in the world do this. For example, the Boston Fire Department has a one-year residency requirement prior to examination date, and the FDNY requires you to be a resident of New York. A residency requirement of one year prior to the examination is a great idea. What a better way than this to leave your mark as the first female Fire Chief of San Francisco. I really hope that you will please take this into consideration, and I really look forward to hearing from you. Thank you.

My commentary for you to learn from:

- WTF? And I don't mean, "Where's The Fire," or "Well Trained Firefighters."
- Wow, I don't know if I would ever have the courage (stupidity?) to send such a letter, let alone any letter to the Fire Chief of a department I was applying for, especially such a big-city fire department – unless it was a thank you letter or a complimentary letter. Does he honestly think that Chief Hayes-White honestly has the time to address such issues that really are only an issue to the frustrated candidate? If you haven't figured it out, most (if not every) Fire Chief is extremely busy and the last thing they need is a letter like such from a candidate. Granted, their administrative staff would probably first screen this and may or may not even get it to the Fire Chief.
- Had he done his research (homework), he would have realized San Francisco used to have a residency requirement. From 1988 to 1999, San Francisco was under a Federal Consent Decree,

meaning they had to hire one minority for every one white male because of the past inequities in their hiring process. During this timeframe, they also had a residency requirement to live within the City and County limits of San Francisco.

- In most Cities and/or Counties, especially in such big cities like San Francisco, a Fire Chief alone does not have the authority to even make such a change. Such changes must go through a lengthy process, with numerous levels of government and bureaucracy being involved. The City leadership (Mayor, Council) will want their say. The Union leadership will want their say (they'll fight it to allow their members to not be tied to living in such a small area). The Fire Commission (if any – yes in this case) will want their say. The County Board of Supervisors will want their say. Then of course the courts will more than likely get involved because in most places, living requirements for public safety personnel have usually been shot down and determined unconstitutional. Based on all that red tape, do you think the Chief wants to take on that battle? If you look at all the other things she has on her plate at any give time (no different than any other Fire Chief), I would say she has much more important issues to address. Pick your battles as they say.
- I get the reason to have living requirements; it allows personnel to have less stress commuting to work; it allows personnel to come back in an emergency sooner and if at all than if they live a few hours away or a few states away; it allows them to take more ownership in the community they get paid by. But I also get the drawbacks: affordable housing, lack of quality schools, etc.

Fire Service Career Opportunities

Most of you are probably reading this book because you want to be a firefighter, and that is great. However, realize there are many different opportunities in the fire service for people to work in. Many people might disagree with this statement, but I truly believe not everyone is cut out to become a firefighter. Some things in life are just not obtainable; I hate to sound negative, but it is true. For example, you want to become a firefighter, but you have a hearing deficit. That may keep you from being a firefighter. Or, you find out that you don't like the blood and guts that we occasionally see on medical calls. Or, you get into your first training live burn and find out you really don't like being that close to the fire or that you're claustrophobic in your self-contained breathing apparatus. All of those things are possible and happen on a regular basis.

Even if you don't want to become a firefighter, realize there are many other excellent career opportunities still available to you. My wife is a great example. She loves the fire prevention and fire investigation side of things while I love the fire suppression side of things. She would rather prevent the fires from occurring and then as a last resort, determine what caused them after they have occurred. She still can't understand why I would have more fun going into a burning building. However, the common thread is that we both enjoy working in the fire service, and there are different opportunities for both of us to make a career out of and have fun doing.

Different Titles / Ranks of Fire Service Personnel:

Firefighter Recruit/Firefighter Trainee/ Firefighter Entry: what some departments call their entry-level firefighters who are assigned to their recruit academy. Once they graduate the academy and/or the probationary period, they will become a Firefighter. The term recruit or trainee typically means you are on probation, may or may not have union representation, are probably paid at a reduced rate, and maybe have little or no benefits. Many departments do this as a cost-saving measure, since until you have completed the academy or probation, you have yet to prove yourself and may or may not be someone that successfully makes it to a Firefighter position.

Firefighter: some departments hire people as firefighters, even if they are going to be put through a fire academy and are going to have to complete a probationary period. Every department is different. Fire apparatus are typically staffed by one company officer (also known as Captain or Lieutenant); one driver (also known as Engineer or Apparatus Operator); and at least one Firefighter (some have more than one firefighter). The firefighter typically rides "backwards" or in the back portion of the cab (behind the driver and the company officer).

Firefighter/Engineer: some departments (like the one I work for) do not have the rank of Engineer, or dedicated driver of the apparatus. Our administration (like many others) has determined that they want all firefighters to be able to drive the fire apparatus. They feel it provides more flexibility and a better-trained staff. A firefighter/engineer typically rotates driving and riding backwards as a firefighter.

Engineer, Apparatus Operator or Driver: the person who drives and operates the apparatus. Typically to become an engineer in most departments, a person has to have been a firefighter for anywhere from two to five years, and then take a competitive promotional examination and successfully pass all of the components of the examination (written test, practical examination) to get promoted. To some fire service personnel, the position of Engineer is the best one in the department. Not every department has assigned drivers. Some departments utilize a senior firefighter to drive the apparatus. Some departments use multiple terms; for example, the Los Angeles Fire Department utilizes Engineers to drive the engines and Apparatus Operators to drive the trucks.

Company Officer, Captain, or Lieutenant: the person who is typically in charge of an apparatus (engine or truck company) and has the responsibility of supervising and training a crew of two to three members (one Engineer and one or two firefighters). In most departments, a person is eligible to test for the position of company officer after they have been on the department for anywhere from three to seven years. The company officer is the first-level supervisor within the fire service, one of the most critical positions on the department. Many departments are now requiring persons wishing to promote to company officer to possess at least a two-year degree.

Battalion Chief or District Chief: the person who is in charge of a number of fire stations and fire companies on a specific shift (such as A, B, or C shift). Typically, a person can test for the position of Battalion Chief / District Chief after having been a company officer for anywhere between two and four years. Most Battalion Chiefs work a 24-hour schedule; however, it is common to also see Battalion Chiefs work a 40-hour schedule in various administrative positions within the training, operations, fire prevention, or support services divisions of a department. Many departments are now requiring persons who wish to promote to battalion chief to possess at least a four-year degree.

Division Chief: the person typically working a 40 hour week at headquarters and in charge of a division such as training, operations, fire prevention or support services. Many departments are now requiring persons who wish to promote to division chief to possess at least a four-year degree.

Deputy Chief: the person typically working a 40 hour week at headquarters and in charge of a division such as training, operations, fire prevention or support services (similar to division chief; some departments only have division chiefs or deputy chiefs, larger departments have both). Some departments call the person directly underneath the Fire Chief, the Assistant Chief, and some departments call the person directly underneath the Fire Chief, the Deputy Chief.

Many departments are now requiring persons who wish to promote to deputy chief to possess at least a four-year degree.

Assistant Chief: the person typically working a 40-hour week at headquarters and overseeing the deputy, division, and / or battalion chiefs (depending on the size of the department and the number of chief officers). Some departments call the person directly underneath the Fire Chief, the Assistant Chief, and some departments call the person directly underneath the Fire Chief, the Deputy Chief. Many departments are now requiring persons who wish to promote to assistant chief to possess at least a four-year degree.

Fire Chief: the person ultimately in charge of all aspects of the fire department. The Chief Executive Officer (CEO) of the fire department. The Fire Chief typically reports to the City Manager if working for a City Fire Department, or the County Executive if working for a County Fire Department. Many departments are now requiring persons who wish to promote to fire chief to possess at least a four-year degree, with a master's degree preferred.

Fire Prevention Related Opportunities:

Fire Investigator: only large departments can typically afford to have a person dedicated to just performing cause and origin investigation for fires. Most departments have fire inspectors, fire marshals, firefighters, or captains perform these duties in addition to their regular duties. If a person is just a fire investigator, they typically are the rank of firefighter, engineer, or captain.

Fire Inspector: the person responsible for performing fire and life safety inspections at the commercial occupancies within a jurisdiction, typically filled with either a civilian employee, or someone of the rank of firefighter or engineer from within the department. This is also typically the entry-level fire prevention bureau position in most departments; this person may or may not also provide fire investigation duties.

Deputy Fire Marshal: the person responsible for performing fire and life safety inspections at the commercial occupancies within a jurisdiction. Typically either a civilian employee, or someone of the rank of firefighter, engineer, or company officer; many or may not also provide fire investigation duties.

Senior Deputy Fire Marshal: the person responsible for supervising fire inspectors and/or deputy fire marshals, and usually found in larger departments requiring additional levels of supervision, due to the number of fire inspectors and/or deputy fire marshals.

Assistant Fire Marshal: the person directly underneath the Fire Marshal, supervising a number of fire inspectors, deputy fire marshals, or senior deputy fire marshals. The person filling this rank is typically the rank of battalion chief or equivalent. Larger departments will tend to have this additional level of supervision, due to the number of fire inspectors and / or deputy fire marshals.

Fire Marshal: the person overseeing the fire prevention division, typically the rank of battalion chief, division chief, deputy chief, or assistant chief, depending on the structure of the department.

NOTE: Any of the above positions may be considered "sworn" or "non-sworn." Someone who is sworn is typically also qualified to be a firefighter (could be of any rank) to work on the "line," meaning out of a fire station. Non-sworn personnel are usually civilians who are not trained in fire suppression duties and usually do not come from the firefighter ranks. Some departments choose to staff various administrative positions with non-sworn or civilian personnel to reduce costs, as a civilian employee typically does not get paid as much as a sworn person, and typically receives a lower level of benefits.

Training Related Opportunities:

Firefighter: many departments, especially larger ones, have a firefighter (or multiple firefighters) assigned to the training division, to assist with teaching classes and preparing training curriculum.

Captain: many departments have a captain or lieutenant (or multiple captains and/or lieutenants) assigned to the training division to assist with teaching classes, preparing training curriculum, and/or coordinating the training division.

Training Officer: the person who is overseeing the training division.

This person could be a captain, battalion chief, division chief, deputy chief, or an assistant chief.

Other Related Opportunities:

Public Education Officer: the person dedicated to ensuring that public education is being provided to the citizens protected by the department. Larger departments typically have one (or more) person assigned to this position on a 40 hour work week, typically of a firefighter, engineer, or company officer rank. Smaller departments typically have an individual of the same rank perform these duties, but on a shift schedule and in addition to their regular firefighting duties.

Public Information Officer (PIO): the person dedicated to promoting the department through the media, in both emergency and non-emergency situations. Typically the PIO is a company officer level position, working a 40 hour work week and on-call nights and weekends. Many large departments have one person dedicated to this position, while smaller departments utilize personnel on shift (firefighters, engineers, company officers, etc.).

Mechanic: the person responsible for maintaining the fire apparatus and support vehicles. Mechanics are typically hired from outside the fire department and without a firefighting background. Mechanics typically work 40 hour work weeks and either work for the fire department or the city fleet maintenance shop, and usually only perform mechanic duties.

Fire Dispatcher: the person responsible for taking the 911 call, processing the 911 call, and ensuring the assigned fire apparatus complete their mission successfully. Some departments hire civilian dispatchers and some department allow firefighters to work as dispatchers.

NOTE: Ranks and positions can vary depending on the size and budget of the fire department. A good rule of thumb is that the bigger the fire department, the more opportunities for advancement and specialty assignments.

8 Reasons People Never Get Hired As Firefighters

On one hand, becoming a firefighter is not an easy task. On the other hand, it is not impossible or out of reach to become a firefighter, if you have properly prepared yourself. Remember, life is about choices. Only you can make the difference in your life and what you make of your life.

Becoming a firefighter is something that many people start out pursuing. Unfortunately the majority of those people probably never achieve their dream of becoming a full-time, paid firefighter. Why is that? I believe there are many reasons why people never achieve that dream, and I plan to discuss those reasons so that you can never find yourself in the position of saying, "If only I had tried harder, if only I had not done that stupid thing that got me in trouble with the law, if only I had better prepared myself; I might have become a firefighter."

Why do people that set out to become a firefighter, never achieve that dream? Here are the 8 reasons I believe that keep people from obtaining their dream of becoming a firefighter:

1. It never truly is a dream.
2. They do not take the process seriously.
3. They are not doing all of the things they should be doing to prepare themselves.
4. They cannot admit their own weaknesses, and subsequently be able to do something about those weaknesses.

5. They are not able to take constructive criticism.
6. They continue to make excuses why they are not getting hired.
7. They cannot pass the necessary phases of the hiring process.
8. They just simply give up.

Let me now go into some details on each of the above reasons, so that you can hopefully prevent yourself from being in that positions someday.

Reason #1: It never truly is a dream.

To become a firefighter, nobody says it is something you have to have wanted to do since you were a little child. While that makes for an interesting story during an oral interview, it is something that is almost unrealistic today. I bet every department has excellent firefighters that only became interested in the career while they were in their adult years and learned of the position after hearing about what a firefighter does from a friend or relative, or from a firefighter at a recruitment drive.

What I am getting at here is that I believe it doesn't matter how long you have wanted to become a firefighter, what matters is how serious you are about becoming a firefighter, and how much you make that into a dream. Anyone that has a passion for something is going to have a better chance at succeeding than someone who is just going through the motions, or not taking every day as an opportunity to get closer to achieving their dream.

Reason #2: They do not take the process seriously.

Becoming a firefighter is not something you can expect to obtain when you only take a couple of tests per year, when you do not make the attempt at updating your resume at last once a month, or when you do not live, eat, and breathe the entire process. I believe it is a full-time job just getting a firefighter position. You truly need to be in it for the long haul.

When candidates first start out, they are usually appearing to be very motivated. Then some of them get sidetracked and lose their focus. They find a significant other. Their significant other they presently have is not prepared for what they are actually getting themselves into, having to wait a few years for you to get hired. They find out it is not what they truly want to do. They get discouraged after taking a couple of tests and not doing so well.

Take every test you are qualified to take. Think about creative ways to improve your resume on a monthly basis whether it completing another certificate, performing more volunteer community service hours, or completing another fire related class. Live, eat, and breathe the entire process. Those that take things very seriously, and make a sincere and dedicated effort at becoming a firefighter, stand an excellent chance when compared to those that do not make the effort to learn everything they can about the field they want to get into and spend the rest of their life in.

Reason #3: They are not doing all of the things they should be doing to prepare themselves.

Remember, if something isn't working the first time, how many times do you have to do the same thing over and over again before you realize you might need to move on to plan b, or plan c? I know it is one thing to try something that doesn't work the first time, and then try it a second time. After about the third time, you need to step back, regroup and look at some alternatives. I am amazed at the people that just keep on doing the same things (without trying something different), and then wonder why they are not getting hired. "If it isn't broke, don't fix it," is a phrase you should be thinking of. If you're not getting hired, then you need to fix something!

Reason #4: They cannot admit their own weaknesses, and are subsequently unable able to do something about those weaknesses.

Regardless of what your mother might tell you, we all have

weaknesses. That is why we are human beings. We are not perfect. As soon as you admit that and are aware of your weaknesses and the areas that need improving, you are showing your maturity and ability to grow – both personally and professionally. If I had a dollar for all the times I heard "It's not me, it's them," I would be rich. Remember, there are at least two sides to every story. We appear to live in a society that has forgotten the words responsibility and accountability.

Have you ever watched the T.V. show COPS? How many of the folks that get arrested actually admit to what they did wrong? Very few! Start taking accountability and responsibility for yourself in everything you do, including when you are in the process of becoming a firefighter. This includes knowing and admitting to your weaknesses and shortcomings. If you always think you are the one that is correct and do not need to change the way you are doing something, approaching something, or interacting with someone, then you will limit yourself in regards to personal development and career development.

Reason #5: They are not able to take constructive criticism.

If you are not able to take constructive criticism now during the hiring process, how are you going to succeed as a firefighter? Being a firefighter subjects someone to criticism their entire career; during the academy, during probation, during the promotional process, as a firefighter, as an officer, as a public servant, etc. Like it or not, we are in the public eye and are always subject to criticism now. If you cannot take it now, and learn from your mistakes and correct your weaknesses, how are you ever going to grow, mature, and better yourself as a fire service professional?

Reason #6: They continue to make excuses why they are not getting hired.

While on vacation a few years ago down in Southern California, I met a guy who was working at this fire museum as a volunteer while also working as a paid-call firefighter and trying to become a full-time paid firefighter. We started talking about the local big-city department. I had asked him if he worked for that department since he was working in the museum. He told me no.

After a little conversation, he started making excuses about why he had not been hired there. He started going into how the department had "lowered their standards," hired "unqualified individuals who didn't deserve to be hired," and then went on how he was "getting passed over and discriminated against because he was a white male." Out of curiosity, I asked him why he thought he was better than those candidates who had been hired. He went on to say how he was a firefighter-1 and EMT, had been a volunteer and paid-call firefighter for almost six years, and had paid his dues, and so on.

Now fifteen years ago, I might have actually had some sympathy for him. Instead, I asked him, "Have you thought of going to paramedic school?" He said he shouldn't have to. I then asked him if he had a two-year degree or a four-year degree. He said no, and that the "fire departments aren't looking for college kids." I then asked him if he spoke a second language. He said no. I then asked him what he had done volunteering in his community besides firefighting. He said nothing. I asked him what his short range, medium range, and long range goals were in regards to becoming a firefighter, of which he answered "I'll keep on plugging away until I get the job, somebody will eventually hire me."

Now I don't know about you, but I don't want to go through life without a specific game plan of what to do or road map of how to get there. Will he ever get hired? Good question. Maybe he will get lucky; maybe he will never achieve that dream. Until he changes his way of thinking and stops making excuses for what he cannot do as opposed to making plans for what he can do, he will probably not get too far.

Reason #7: They cannot pass the necessary phases of the hiring process.

I know this sounds obvious, but if you cannot pass all of the phases of the hiring process, you will not get the job! Many candidates just prepare themselves for one specific event, such as the written exam, the physical ability test, or the oral interview. While all of those are important, and you do usually have to pass one phase to move onto the next phase, you need to spend time preparing for all of the phases. How do you get better at taking tests? By taking as many tests as you can!

Think of every test as that one that is preparing you to do the best you can when you are participating in the hiring process for your dream department. Learn from your mistakes so you can improve in the future. If you are not passing the written exam, or at least scoring 90%, take a serious look at what your weak areas might be and what you need to do to improve those scores. If you are not passing physical ability tests, either begin a physical fitness routine, or change your present physical fitness routine so that it is working on your weaknesses. If you are not scoring in the top 10% of the final candidate pool after your oral interview, take a look in the mirror and realize the problem might be you, not the oral board.

Personally, the written examination and the physical ability tests are the no-brainers. They just get you in the door to participate in the oral interview. The oral interview is where the rubber meets the road. This is where you get hired. That 10 to 30 minute interview is what makes you or breaks you. You can have the best resume in the world but if you can't sell yourself or communicate effectively during the oral interview, chances are you won't get the job.

Reason #8: They just simply give up.

Remember, once you give up at something – you never have the chance to find out if you ever could have accomplished what you originally set out to accomplish. How long does it take to become a firefighter? There is no set formula or time frame. What works for one person, might not work for another. I truly believe there is a firefighter position for everyone out there who does not give up at obtaining their dream. I'm not saying everyone is meant to be a firefighter or cut out to be a firefighter. I'm saying that if you stick with this process long enough and remain focused, and make yourself the best candidate you can be, you will eventually become a firefighter.

The probationary process is what will hopefully weed out the folks that are not cut out to be firefighters. Sometimes the hiring process alone is not enough to determine how well a candidate will perform once they are given the job. Sometimes it takes a few years after a firefighter has completed probation to find out they are not cut out to be a firefighter, and that happens from time-to-time. The hiring process is by no means perfect, and it is entirely possible for a candidate to slide their way into a firefighter position and potentially pass probation. I bet most fire departments nationwide have at least one firefighter that has completed probation that makes their fellow firefighters wonder, "how did this person ever get hired" or "why is this person a firefighter, they don't seem to be cut out for the job?" Welcome to reality.

Some might get the badge on the first test while others might have to take 100 tests. Some might only spend less than a year at the process, while others might take 10-15 years to become a firefighter. A few years ago, my department hired a candidate who had been testing for 13 years! Could he have been hired earlier? Of course he could have. He had just fallen into the trap of feeling sorry for himself, not believing in himself, and committing some of the other reasons why people never achieve their dream. While he eventually landed his dream job, had he stuck to a plan and maybe been more serious about the overall process, he would have obtained his badge many years ago and not had to deal with all of the stress of not achieving his dream.

Candidates ask me what are their chances of actually getting hired. I tell them it is simple. No one can guarantee their getting hired. However, if they never give up and they continue preparing themselves in every possible way, continue improving their knowledge, skills, and abilities every chance they have, and keep focused, they stand a really good chance at getting hired. Does everyone get hired? No. But those that stick it out stand the best chance. I've known many people that have been hired after having tested for over ten years. I've never known anyone to get hired once they gave up their dream and stopped trying to become a firefighter.

If you truly believe that becoming a firefighter is a dream of yours, then by all means pursuit that dream! Many people talk the talk, but how many actually walk the walk? It is not easy becoming a firefighter. However, if you realize that you must be in this for the long haul, that it might take you a few years, that it is a full-time job just becoming a firefighter, and that you need to not find yourself falling into one of the 8 reasons why people never achieve their dream of becoming a firefighter, I sincerely believe you will be on your way to achieving your dream.

50 Character Traits A Firefighter Candidate Should Possess

There is no, one-size fits all candidate, that is a best fit for a fire department. However, there are numerous character traits that are considered to be highly desirable by many departments when they are evaluating candidates during the hiring process and especially during the oral interview process. If you work for a fire department and are responsible for hiring, training, and/or evaluating firefighters, do you have a way to adequately test a candidate for the following traits? If not, I encourage you to find a way to do so.

If you work for a fire department that is having a problem with a specific probationary firefighter or has had a track record of having problems with probationary firefighters, take a look at the list below and I will bet those firefighters did not possess a good majority of them. If that is the case, see if there is a way to evaluate for these character traits before you put someone into the recruit academy and/or probation, and have already invested a significant amount of money to getting them up and running. Being proactive is always preferred to being reactive.

Here are some positive character traits a successful candidate will be able to demonstrate and discuss with the oral board and the fire department that is evaluating whether you will be a good fit for their department:

1. **Accountable** (for your actions, your performance, etc.).

2. **Adaptable** (to pretty much any situation or task asked of you).

3. **Advocate** (for your customer, knowing when to do the right thing for the right reason).

4. **Aggressiveness** (not in a dangerous or stupid way, but in a positive and safe way. Aggressive in your pursuit of education and training, in your way of doing the best job you can, etc.).

5. **Caring** (for your customers and co-workers).

6. **Commitment** (to life-long learning and education, to the fire service, to your department, to your customers).

7. **Common sense** (face it, people with a lack of common sense helps keep us employed. A firefighter that lacks common sense is useless in my opinion).

8. **Compassionate** (to your customers and co-workers).

9. **Customer service oriented** (everything we do is for the customer. If it weren't for them, we would not have jobs).

10. **Dedication** (to the fire service, your department, your career, your co-workers, and to your customers).

11. **Dependable** (showing up early and always on time, never late or forgetting to do something or be somewhere).

12. **Disciplined** (knowing when to say when, what to do, and what not to do).

13. **Diversity friendly** (appreciation of and understanding of).

14. **Driven** (to success, to better your performance, to be the best you can be, to serve your customer the best you can, etc.).

15. **Empathy** (to your customers and co-workers).

16. **Ethics** (what do you think is ethical behavior? Every day you will be faced with making ethical decisions; all it takes is one poor choice and your career or reputation is ruined).

17. **Faith** (not necessarily in a religious way, but that things will get better and that your superiors are acting in your best interest).

18. **Flexible** (to pretty much any situation or task asked of you).

19. **Good listener** (if you're talking more than you're listening, you're probably not a good communicator).

20. **Hard-worker** (the world has enough slackers and slot fillers. Be the one that is the last to sit down and the first one to get

up and do the work needing to be done. Also, be the one that doesn't complain about having to do things when they need to get done).

21. **Honesty** (to your department, to your customers, and to your co-workers).

22. **Honor** (to the fire service, to your department, to your customers, and to your co-workers).

23. **Humorous** (a sense of humor is critical to your success and enjoyment of life. You have to be able to make fun of yourself, tell clean jokes that do not offend anyone, not take things personally, have thick skin, and be able to make the best out of the worst situation).

24. **Initiative** (we want folks that know what to do and when to do it. Don't wait to be told to do something, it may be too late and you'll already have earned a reputation of being a slacker or being lazy).

25. **Integrity** (as a representative of the department, off duty and on duty, we want folks that will represent us in the best light. Positive public relations are vital to our survival).

26. **Intelligence** (we don't need to hire a dummy. We expect you to hit the ground running and provide educated opinions and make smart decisions when needed).

27. **Lack of ego** (there is a fine line between being confident and cocky. We want confidence; we don't want cockiness. Everyone has an ego – make sure yours doesn't get in the way of doing the right thing for the right reason).

28. **Lack of entitlement** (the fire department and the fire service were here long before you were; it will also be here long after you are dead and gone. You are not entitled to anything, not even a job. Appreciate what you have and respect each day you are fortunate enough to work in the greatest industry in the world – the fire service).

29. **Leadership** (management and leadership do not mean the same thing. Personnel of all ranks and seniority need to demonstrate leadership ability on a continuous basis in everything they do).

30. **Loyalty** (to your department, your customers, your co-workers).

31. **Maturity** (age doesn't determine maturity, character does).

32. **Motivation** (only you can motivate yourself, don't expect someone else to have to do so, it cannot happen).

33. **Organized** (if you want to be a firefighter and especially if you want to ever be a company or chief officer, you have to be organized. Not being organized will increase stress and cause you to not get as much accomplished, as you would like to or need to).

34. **Obedience** (to your department, to the fire service, to your customers, to your co-workers).

35. **Passion** (towards your department, towards the fire service, towards your customers, towards your co-workers).

36. **Persistence** (in everything you do, don't be a quitter).

37. **Punctual** (you are expected to be early – at least on time, to all phases of the hiring process and when you are working as a firefighter. Tardiness is unacceptable and will lead to discipline if not corrected or controlled. When you call 9-1-1, do you want the emergency crews to be on time, early, or late?).

38. **Responsible** (for yourself, your actions, your performance, etc.).

39. **Retention** (ability to retain things. You don't want to be the person with the nickname "50 first dates" after the movie of the same name. That would tend to make someone believe you don't remember things after you are told or taught something).

40. **Sacrifices** (ability to make sacrifices for the betterment of your department, the fire service, your family, your customers, your co-workers, etc.).

41. **Self-confidence** (there is a fine line between being too confident and too cocky. We love confidence; we hate cockiness. Taking a blood pressure and letting the paramedic know that "I think it is about 120/80" does not demonstrate self-confidence. "The blood pressure is 120/80" demonstrates self-confidence).

42. **Self-starter** (you can't always wait to be told how or when to do something. Sometimes you need to get something done and at the right time. Waiting for your company officer to tell you

to do your assigned housework everyday means you are not a self-starter and lack initiative).

43. **Studious** (becoming a firefighter is like learning a new language. You will be learning something new everyday on the job. If you are not, something is wrong. There is a difference between having 30 years of experience on the job and 30 "1 year experiences combined for a total of 30 years.").

44. **Sympathy** (to your customers, to your co-workers).

45. **Talkative** (not in a negative or annoying way, but having the ability to talk about yourself and communicate with others. Since we work closely with others, for 24 hours or more at a time, we want to get to know our co-workers, especially the new ones. Be able to talk about yourself in a tactful and non-overbearing, yet interesting way that makes people want to be around you).

46. **Teamwork** (face it, there is no "I" in team. One person cannot do this job by themselves. The fire service does not need loners; we need people that can fit into a team, accomplish work through teamwork, and work harmoniously with various people from all genders and ethnicities).

47. **Tenacity** (at whatever you are doing).

48. **Trustworthiness** (trust in your department, trust in your co-workers, and the ability to demonstrate trust in your actions and words).

49. **Work ethic** (slackers need not apply to a career in the fire service. You need a good work ethic; having one will earn you a great reputation and help you when it comes to paying your dues).

50. **Values** (what are yours – what do you stand for and think is appropriate behavior?).

You may think that I have duplicated many of the items because they sound similar. While many traits are similar, they are also different in many ways. Please take the time to learn and understand what each word means and have a good example of how you are currently living up to that word and how you intend to be that way in the future. Doing so will not only make you a better person, but also a better firefighter – someone anyone would be proud to say they know and work with.

Basic Questions To Ask Before Starting

Before you get started, you should really take a look in the mirror and make a self-evaluation that is honest, critical, and objective. Why should you do this? To get a better idea of what will be your greatest challenges you will have to overcome to become a firefighter.

Question #1: What do you see as your biggest weakness in getting hired as a firefighter?

Understanding what your biggest weaknesses are will greatly increase your odds of becoming a firefighter, and also shorten your length of job hunting. Face it, most of us do not like to think we have weaknesses, and definitely don't want to hear them from other folks (known as constructive criticism). I definitely don't like to find out I have weaknesses, especially from other people. However, if I don't listen to what others are saying or take the time to perform a self-evaluation to determine my weaknesses, I'm never going to improve those weaknesses. Never improving my weaknesses can have potential future harm in areas such as personal relationships, promotions, friendships, etc.

Being able to listen to what others are saying and actually take their opinions to heart (and not take them personally), and then put them into a plan of action for improvement, will do wonders for you, including increasing your chances of getting hired or promoted. It seems like a day does not go by where I have the opportunity to talk with a person interested in a fire service career. I am very willing to offer my opinion, especially when they ask me for it. The only thing I usually warn them, is to be careful what you ask for. Many candidates don't like hearing the truth (or at least the perceived truth) about them. Remember Jack Nicholson's line to Tom Cruise in the movie "A few good men?" "You want the truth? You can't handle the truth." There is definitely some truth to that statement.

Don't take what people say to you in the way of constructive criticism as being a personal attack. Most folks don't say things for you to take personally; they say them to let you know what they perceive about you. If they are taking the time to tell you their opinion, it is probably worth hearing. If they perceive something to be worth changing, don't you think many other people are also probably thinking the same thing? Also, just because someone doesn't provide you with constructive criticism, doesn't mean they aren't thinking about it. Many people just hate conflict, or don't want to waste their time on you for whatever reason.

Question #2: What is your greatest strength that will assist you in becoming a firefighter?

It is as important to know your strengths, as it is to know your weaknesses when it comes to becoming a firefighter. Knowing your strengths can help you succeed, especially if you capitalize on them. My strengths were my motivation, my dependability, and my passion for the job. I made sure I talked about those strengths whenever I participated in an oral interview. I also provided examples to back up why I thought each of those were strengths. Additionally, those strengths helped me get hired because I did not give up, I was able to remain focused, and I was able to live, eat, and breathe the fire service.

Question #3: What do you see as your greatest challenge in getting hired as a firefighter?

Some people will be very quick to pull the race card on this subject, especially white males. I'll be honest, I used to think that way, until I finally came to the realization that white males are still getting hired, many of them with just EMT certificates, and some of them with minimal fire or EMS education / experience.

I'll give an example. One of the big-city fire departments in California hires people off the top of the list. Meaning, if they have ten openings, then numbers one through ten are the first to get job offers (assuming they have passed all of the phases of the hiring process). It doesn't matter what qualifications you have, if the oral board determined you performed exceptionally well, then you had a great chance at making the top of the list. I was seeing white males getting hired with less education or experience than I had! Why, because they had obviously prepared for their oral interview more than I had. Before you think the department had lowered their standards and/or hired unqualified candidates, think again. Most of those candidates have typically succeeded to become competent firefighters.

This is almost unheard of in many departments. Most big-city fire departments allow the fire chief to pick from the entire list or at least use the rule of three, five or even ten when it comes to selecting candidates. For example, one use of the rule of three is if there are two positions to hire, the Fire Chief will have to interview the top four candidates and is only able to hire out of those four candidates (either #1, #2, #3, and/or #4). Another use of the rule of the rule of three is to times the number of positions to hire by three. So if a Fire Chief was going to hire two people, he/she could interview six people and choose his/her two from those six. The rule of five, ten or whatever number usually works the same. So, being number one on some department's lists doesn't hold that much weight, especially when the Fire Chief has the liberty to select whoever they want off of the list, to best meet the needs of the department and the community.

While there may be some truth to that statement, depending on the department or the community, I personally don't see it as a major challenge; definitely not as much of a major challenge that many candidates make it out to be. While the jury is still out on whether this is still a major challenge, realize if this describes you, there is nothing you can do about it. Don't become bitter or give up; get over it, and do what you have to do in other areas of your preparation to make up for it (become a paramedic, work on your oral interview skills, become bilingual, etc.).

Another challenge many candidates face is that they just don't qualify to take the test for a specific department. If you look at the history of many departments, they typically only hire (or allow to apply and participate in the testing process) candidates with specific qualification such as EMT, paramedic, firefighter 1 certificate and/or academy, bilingual ability, etc. If a department only hires candidates with specific qualifications, and you do not possess those qualifications, then you will probably never get hired by that department. Seems pretty obvious to me that you need to do some research on the different departments you desire to work for and see what their track record of hiring consists of so you can properly prepare yourself.

Question #4: Are you willing to participate in the process of becoming a firefighter for potentially three to five years (more or less)?

Many candidates get into the firefighter testing process without realizing how difficult it is to get hired. Many candidates don't realize how intense the competition is, and how dedicated and focused a candidate must be. When I was testing, I remember hearing that it typically takes someone three to five years to become a full-time firefighter, and I think that still holds true today. Some do it in less time (even after their first test), some take more than five years, and some never get hired.

It took me four and a half years to become a full-time firefighter. I had a four-year degree, a two-year degree, my paramedic license, my firefighter 1 certificate, extensive certifications, numerous hours of community service experience and various other fire service and non-fire service related experience to offer. Are you willing to spend four and a half years? Not everybody is. Many people give up before they even take their first test or right after they take their first test. I teach the Introduction to Fire Technology class at the college, and I usually start out with about 50 students every semester, and typically graduate only about 12 to 20 students. What happened to the other students who started but didn't finish?

Many give up, many realize this was not what they thought it would be, many realize they need more time to prepare, and many realize the job of a firefighter does not contain much actual time of firefighting (since EMS calls make up a good portion of most department's responses).

Occasionally I will see some of the students who have dropped out (or I have dropped out) of my class reappear the next semester, telling me that they needed to take time off for personal reasons or to better prepare themselves for what they were getting into (after having realized it wasn't as easy as they thought it would be). The key to these folks is that they did not give up, that they realized it was not going to be easy, and that they regrouped to get themselves better focused.

Before you get turned off by the idea of having to stick with something for three to five years (without any guarantees of ever getting hired), think of it this way; anything worth having in life takes work, and does not come easy. I was willing to spend five years to become a firefighter because I knew it would be a great career that I could hopefully work in for the next 25 to 35 years.

Think of it another way. If you wanted to become a lawyer, it would probably take you at least three years of law school (in addition to other formal education), and then you would have to pass the BAR exam, which over half of the people fail the first time they take it, and some never pass. Say you wanted to become a Doctor. That would take you about eight years of schooling and hard work, and would leave you with no guarantees of ever becoming a Doctor and with large amounts of student loans to repay. Very few rewarding and challenging careers are obtained in less than two or three years. In some ways, consider yourself lucky and fortunate if you get hired in less than three years from the day you decided to take the testing process seriously. That's why three to five years doesn't look too bad in the grand scheme of things.

Question #5: How bad do you want to become a firefighter?

Most candidates don't get hired after taking just one test or by taking a test just for the fun of it. Most candidates get hired because they seriously want to become a firefighter, and work the next 25 to 35 years in the fire service. Occasionally, I will hear a firefighter say they got hired on their first test and that they really didn't want to become a firefighter, they just took the test because their friends were taking the test, or they thought it would be a fun job to work at for a few years and then go on to something else.

That statement is almost an insult to the many candidates that have spent countless hours and made considerable sacrifices to become firefighters. If that is you, do yourself a favor and don't brag to others that you got hired on your first test or that you just consider the job to be something fun to work at for a while. It will be a good way of alienating yourself and of making you stand out in a negative way from the rest of the firefighters, most of who had to work at getting their badge.

You have to want to become a firefighter bad enough to do whatever it takes (within legal, ethical, and moral reasons) to become a firefighter. If it means getting your EMT certificate, so be it. If it means going through a college firefighter 1 academy, so be it. If it means going through paramedic school, so be it. If it means spending as many waking hours as you can improving yourself and better preparing yourself, so be it. If it means sacrificing time from your family and friends to take tests or better prepare yourself, so be it. Just a word of caution though: remember your family comes first! Don't completely abandon them during your pursuit of becoming a firefighter; they might not be there when you finally get hired and be unable to pin your badge on you at your graduation ceremony. Wouldn't that be a tragedy – you finally got hired as a firefighter by your dream department; however, your spouse left you. You can't tell me that has never happened before.

I was lucky; I was single when I was going through the testing process. Being single made it easy to spend as much time as I did preparing myself and taking tests. I could not have done everything I did if I was married, if I had kids, or if I had a serious girlfriend. Not that they wouldn't let me, but I doubt if I would have been able to find a supportive person that would have stayed with me the entire time, waiting for the payoff to occur (which for some, never comes).

If you are married, have kids, and/or have a serious relationship with a significant other, make sure you don't take too much time away from them. Be very up front and educate them on the process. Educate them on what they are getting into; notice I said them? Yes, it is teamwork to get hired. If they are not behind you 100%, something will end up going bad in the long run: the relationship or the career. If possible, put them in touch with other folks in similar situations, especially the spouses of people already working as firefighters so that they can have someone to talk to and someone to help them understand what it is we do and why we do what we do.

Question #6: What makes you unique when compared to the other candidates?

Most candidates think they have to have every possible certificate on their resume and have the best resume to get hired. That is far from the truth in most situations. What gets many people hired is their uniqueness when compared to the other candidates. Many candidates think that when they get their EMT certificate and their firefighter 1 certificate, that they are set. Well, if those two qualifications are the minimum qualifications to take the test, then every candidate in the room is equally qualified with you. Many of them also have formal education in the way of two or four year degrees.

Getting to see the picture? The oral board is interviewing hundreds of candidates, most of whom have very similar qualifications. How do you stand out from the next candidate? Even more important, do you realize why it is important to stand out from the other candidates (in a positive way)? When the fire chief or the oral board has to select the top 1% of the candidates that are on the hiring list or are being interviewed, to continue in the process, who do you think they are going to pick? The ones that have stuck out in a unique and positive way, that's who.

The problem is that most candidates that go through the oral boards are average candidates. Very few are below average or above average. The ones that are above average are the ones that have stuck out in some unique way to the oral panel. Maybe they had excellent oral communications skills. Maybe they had outstanding charisma and an incredible personality. Maybe they were bilingual in a not-so-common language. Maybe they have some different community service experience from the other candidates. Maybe they have some extensive experience in a certain job, and they are able to relate their past experience to their future success as a firefighter. Maybe their reasons for working for that department or for becoming a firefighter are very passionate, sincere, or convincing, when compared to the other candidates. The list goes on and on.

I don't care whether there are 5, 55, 105, or 1,005 candidates testing for a fire department. Each of them is unique in some way from the next candidate. The trick is finding out what is unique about you so you can sell that during your oral interview to make you stand out from the other candidates.

Question #7: Are you willing to accept that it is a full-time job just getting a job?

I am a firm believer that to be successful at something in life, you have to live, eat, sleep, and breathe that something. Learn as much as you can about the testing process. Learn as much as you can about the fire departments you are testing for, especially how one department differs from another department. Be a student of the career you are aspiring to by formally educating yourself, participating in training, certification, and continuing education classes, and by subscribing to trade related publications and mailing lists to stay up-to-date with what is going on and where the future lies in that specific industry.

When I was testing for firefighter positions, I worked a full-time job, I went to school full-time, I took as many tests as I qualified for, I attempted to volunteer as many hours as I could squeeze into my schedule, and I attempted to train and educate myself as much as I could, to ensure I was the best candidate I could be. I was also trying to make and keep connections in the fire service in the way of firefighters of all ranks and from different departments so that I could have a network of mentors to provide me with advice, suggestions, and feedback.

SUMMARY:

You may not know the exact answers to these questions at this moment; that is ok. Even if you think you have all of the answers now, please be open to other answers that you might be made aware of as time progresses. By asking yourself these questions and honestly answering them (while keeping an open mind and not taking these answers personally), you will hopefully make your journey a bit smoother and more enjoyable.

Basic Necessities For The Firefighter Candidate

I liken becoming a firefighter to the television show "Survivor." In many ways, getting hired as a firefighter is survival of the fittest, and not for the faint at heart. Many candidates begin the process; a select few get hired. Why is that you may wonder? Obviously many candidates do not know what they are getting into or realize how tough and challenging (mentally, physically, and financially) it will be to obtain the career of their dreams. The more you can prepare yourself, the better you are going to be. I have provided below a list of basic necessities every firefighter candidate should have in their toolbox to better prepare themselves for the firefighter testing process and the resulting career they are aspiring to.

#1: Computer access.

A candidate needs computer access for two reasons:

- To learn basic computer skills that will be required of them on the job, even as a firefighter.
- To have a working knowledge of programs such as Microsoft Word, Microsoft Excel, Microsoft PowerPoint, Microsoft Outlook, and be able to use either a PC or a Macintosh based system.

#2: Internet access.

Every candidate needs to have Internet access:

- To research fire departments and the fire service.
- To research the city/county/jurisdiction they are applying to.
- To apply for jobs (some departments allow you to do an online job application).
- To network with other candidates and fire service professionals.
- To just be in touch with the latest technology.

#3: Professional email address.

Not having a professional looking and sounding email address in today's world is similar to not owning a vehicle or not having the desire to learn the common language where you work or live. It is a necessity for credibility, respect and the appearance of being mature and professional. I strongly suggest having a professional looking and sounding email address, preferably one that has a form of your name in it, as opposed to something that is hard to read, hard to understand, politically incorrect, or just plain inappropriate, suggestive, and/or immature.

#4: Funding source (legal).

Any career worth having is going to take time, energy, education, and most of all money to obtain. Money will be required to pay for education, pay for travel expenses while taking firefighter examinations, pay for appropriate attire to wear to oral interviews and other phases of the hiring process, and so forth. You have to spend money to make money, and this is no different. Preferably mom and dad are not your primary funding source, nor is a sugar daddy or sugar momma. Why you might ask? Because an oral board does not want to hear that you have lived at home all your life with mom and dad paying for everything. That doesn't prove much in the way of independence, fiscal responsibility, or budgeting on your part. The best funding source is a job (legal and ethical one) that will also provide valuable experience to go on your resume and to sell to an oral board.

#5: Clean presentation.

Even though the world today is not as conservative as it used to be, the fire service, other governmental agencies, and most businesses still look to hire people that present themselves very well, especially in the way of personal grooming, attire, etc. Remember that perception is reality, and if you look like a slob, or look unkempt, then you probably are in the eyes of the beholder.

#6: Transportation.

It is very important to have transportation, and specifically reliable transportation. The last thing you want to have to do is worry about your car not making it to the written examination. If your car breaks down on the way to the test, and you end being late to the test, most departments will not let you continue in the process. While it might seem unfair, it is reality. If you have a vehicle that is not reliable, then you might need to look into alternate means of travel (which may or may not also be reliable) such as friends, public transportation, etc. The problem with those options is that they are subject to breakdowns, traffic delays, availability, overstaying your welcome, etc.

#7: Dress attire.

Males and females need to have at least one (preferably two – in case something happens to the first outfit, if it is in the dry cleaners, or if you have events on back-to-back days and the first outfit is unavailable or dirty) very nice dress outfit in their wardrobe. You will need this outfit for the oral interview, for the chief's interview, and possibly other events of the hiring process. If nothing else, you can always use that outfit for weddings, funerals, dressy events, etc.

#8: Extremely positive attitude.

The fire service is always looking for folks with a positive attitude. Becoming a firefighter can be such a draining, challenging, and depressing process at times that it is easy to get a bad or negative attitude. Been there, done that myself. It can be very depressing at times when you think you did well on a test and you find out just the opposite, or you find out that you missed a testing opportunity because of some reason or another. Regardless, you have to force yourself to stay positive and realize that good things come to those that wait, and are persistent and positive. What's meant to be is meant to be. Having a negative attitude does nobody any good, especially yourself.

#9: Excellent listening skills.

This is a big problem of many people in the world today, not just firefighter candidates. Having excellent listening skills will be beneficial in many ways:

- On the fireground, you must be 100% sure of the orders you are given and what is expected of you.
- During an oral board, the last thing you want to have to do is ask the oral board to repeat a question. That does not demonstrate good listening skills and can actually go against you. On the fireground as the Incident Commander, I do not want to have to continuously repeat my orders. I have better things to do and other priorities to accomplish than wasting valuable time repeating things you did not hear.
- In personal relationships, communication is a continuous problem area. If all of us had excellent listening skills, I truly believe there would be less divorces and less problems overall.
- In the fire station, poor listening skills can and do lead to problems with your co-workers and/or supervisors.

#10: Good character traits.

Good character traits include such words as honesty, trustworthiness, accountability, a sense of responsibility, a good sense of humor, a tolerance of diversity, loyalty, hard-worker, faithful, and dependable, just to name a few. Besides making you a better human being, they will also make you a more successful firefighter and greatly increase your chances of getting hired. Good character traits are evaluated in almost every phase of the hiring process – from the time you file the job application, to the written test, to the oral board, to the psychological examination, to the chief's interview, and to the background investigation. Character traits (good and bad) will come up at all points of the process, and will more than likely help you get the job, or keep you from getting the job. Additionally, good character traits will help you complete the recruit academy, complete probation, and have a successful career as a firefighter.

#11: Common sense.

Contrary to popular belief, common sense is not as common as we think (which is one of the reasons firefighters and police officers have jobs!). We cannot teach you common sense; common sense is something that you are either born with or are able to obtain and continuously improve on during your life. Lack of common sense can keep you from getting hired as a firefighter, and also terminate your employment as a firefighter.

#12: Blue Pen & A Watch (With A Second Hand).

From today on, do not leave home without the following two items: a blue pen and a watch with a second hand. Notice I did not say a smart phone with a timing device. I learned this nugget when I was going through the Chabot College Fire Technology Program and still carry these two items with me today. I buy a box of the Uniball blue pens from the local office supply store, always keeping one clipped to my t-shirt collar, with a spare in the back pocket. Nothing is more embarrassing than having to ask someone to borrow a pen. The blue color helps determine which is the original document and is usually the required color for legal documents.

As a firefighter, you'll be asked on a daily basis to take someone's pulse, not to mention time other events. Second to having to ask someone to borrow their pen, nothing is more embarrassing than having to ask your Captain while on a medical response something to the effect of "can you count from one to fifteen while I take the pulse?" I've seen this more than I care to mention. If you want to be considered a professional, act like one and have the appropriate tools when it's showtime!

SUMMARY:

Having these basic necessities in your toolbox will greatly increase your chances of employment as a firefighter. Nobody is perfect; however the more of these you can have in your back pocket, the more successful you are going to be!

25 Reasons To Not Hire
You As A Firefighter

Before we go much further, let us take the time to see some of the reasons fire departments might not want to hire you. Knowing in advance some of these reasons can help you better focus on what you either need to improve on, or attempt to distance from your past. While you cannot erase your past, you can do your best to demonstrate to a fire department that you have learned from the mistakes you have made, you have not made the same mistakes again, that the mistakes were a long time ago, and that you take responsibility and accountability for your actions or non-actions.

Getting hired as a firefighter is an extremely competitive process. Successfully completing all phases of the hiring process and getting the badge is a feat to be proud of. I would venture that on the average, less than 5% of the candidates applying for a firefighter position with a department are likely to get a badge once the process is said and done. Because the process is so competitive and challenging, a person competing to become a firefighter needs to be aware of some of the reasons that can eliminate them from the hiring process, particularly in the oral interview phase.

I also want to stress right away that while the title of this chapter might sound negative, it is not meant to come across as negative. The intent of this chapter is to have you open your eyes to reality and learn from the mistakes that others have made. Note that these reasons can vary from department to department; some departments are very lenient in what they consider to be enough to disqualify a candidate and some departments are very strict in what they consider to be enough to disqualify a candidate from becoming a firefighter.

25 reasons to not hire you as a firefighter:

Reason #1: You arrive late to any phase of the hiring phase, or you do not show up to any phase of the hiring process.

It never hurts to show up well in advance. Plan ahead and assume there will be traffic or parking problems. If possible, do a test drive in advance to know how long it will take you, find out where to park, and find out where to report. Get a map of the area and make sure your transportation is in tip-top shape. Getting there early allows you time to relax, to get focused, and not be stressed about being late and risking the chance of getting eliminated from the hiring process. Remember, you are one of a great number of candidates applying for the job. Don't expect them to keep you in the process and make any special accommodations for you when there are many others that have arrived on time.

Reason #2: Poor listening skills.

If you fail to hear instructions during a portion of the hiring process, you may neglect to do something you are expected to do or do something you are not expected to do. As a firefighter, you will be given direction throughout the day by your company officer, who is expecting you to listen and complete the direction provided. Failure to listen can lead to firefighter injuries and/or deaths (including your own) on the fireground!

Reason #3: Inability to express self clearly or completely; poor voice control; poor grammar or language skills.

To even make the oral interview, your application first has to make it through the screening process. If your application is full of spelling errors or grammar errors, it should make the round file (trash can). Even if it does allow you to go as far as the oral interview (which is usually 100% of your overall score on the hiring list), the inability to express yourself clearly or completely or having poor voice control is enough to keep you from getting a high score on the oral interview, virtually eliminating you from getting a job.

Reason #4: Poor scholastic record.

Just because you got straight A's in school doesn't mean you'll be a great firefighter. However, barely scraping by doesn't make you look that good either. Many departments require you to keep at least an 80% average on written tests while in the recruit academy. Failure to do so can result in your termination. If you are not obtaining at least an 80% score on your written examinations, how do you think you are going to succeed in a fire academy?

Reason #5: Lack of planning for your career; you have no purpose and/or goals.

Fire departments want to hire people that are not going to be just "slot-fillers." Every department has their share of "slot-fillers" that just show up every day and do not do anything more than they have to. They don't go above and beyond, and they usually have to be told to do things. Fire Captains and Chief Officers love firefighters that are low maintenance, that have a basic understanding of what has to be done, that don't have to be told to do something (especially more than once), and are able to take their own initiative to get things done.

Reason #6: Overemphasis on money; interest only in the best wage or benefit package.

I am a firm believer that you don't mention the words "great benefits and excellent pay" when asked why you want to become a firefighter during the oral interview. Don't get me wrong; I feel I am paid well and have a great benefit package. I just don't think it's appropriate to mention as your number one reason for becoming a firefighter. Instead, think of that unique story to tell the oral board what exactly caused that turning point in your life where you made the decision to become a firefighter.

Reason #7: Poor driving history (accidents, tickets, etc.).

Even if you never want to promote to the rank of Engineer, there is still a great chance the department you are applying for will want you to at least obtain a special driver's license (such as the Class "B" Firefighter license in California) by the end of your probationary period. Some job flyers even specify "must obtain a Class "B" Firefighters license by the end of probation." That means if you don't obtain it, you don't pass probation. If you are having trouble driving your personal vehicle (which is probably a lot smaller than a fire engine), do you think you are going to have an easier time driving a piece of fire apparatus?

Reason #8: You want the position only for a short time; you have no interest in the department or the industry.

Although it is rare, occasionally people do get hired as firefighters and end up quitting before they are eligible for retirement (and for reasons other than medical reasons). I truly think we are a unique career. How many careers today (especially when compared to the business world) do you know where you can work for the same company for 30 or so years, until you retire? Not as many as there used to be. When we hire people, we still anticipate that they will stay until they retire. We put thousands of dollars into training and educating you to be the best firefighter you can be. We expect some form of "return on our investment."

This also goes for candidates that are only taking the position to use as a stepping-stone to get on with another department. While I'm not saying this is right or wrong (because you have to do what is right for you and your family), I am saying not to be surprised when a department doesn't hire you because they feel (for whatever reason) that you are only going to be there for a short time until your "dream department" calls you to offer you a job. This is very common in California right now, especially for paramedics. It seems like paramedics with clean backgrounds can pretty much write their own ticket.

I had to face this many times when I was testing, and I think this was because of my education, training, and experience that I had to offer. I was told by some chiefs that they felt I was "overqualified" since I had a four-year degree and I had a variety of other certifications that typically paid firefighters and captains had. My explanation to them was that I did not feel I was overqualified as much as I was well qualified. I tried to explain that the reason I had completed many of those certification classes was because I had already completed my two-year degree in Fire Technology and I wanted to continue my education, which was true. Some bought it; some did not. The chiefs that typically felt this way were chiefs of small departments, with usually less than five fire stations.

I came to find out the reason many of them felt I was overqualified was because they were actually concerned that they would train me and I would leave them for another department, like other firefighters had done in the past. When I saw their side of the story, I understood why they felt the way they did. When you are the chief of a small department, it is very critical that you hire quality people that you can retain for many years.

I was typically asked the question during chief's level interviews, "so, if we hire you, how long before you leave for a bigger department closer to home that will pay you more money and provide you with more career and promotional opportunities?" I couldn't lie. I had to be honest and state that I could not promise them that I would stay. What I could promise them was that I would try my best to be the best firefighter I could be and that maybe I would like the department and the area so much that I wouldn't want to leave. Give me the chance and I will do the best I can to be an asset to your department. Unfortunately, I knew as soon as I was asked this question, they had already made up their mind against hiring me.

Reason #9: Poor oral communication skills; Inability to express self clearly or completely; poor voice control.

Oral communication skills are an integral part of a firefighter's job. Whether it is on a call or around the fire station, you must be able to effectively communicate. A firefighter is continuously communicating throughout the shift: to their co-workers, to their supervisor, to members of the public on emergency and non-emergency scenes, to members of the public during fire inspections, public education details, etc. The last thing a fire chief wants to have is someone that is shy and does not like being around other people.

Reason #10: Poor written communication skills; poor grammar or language skills.

Even if you never want to promote in the fire service, a firefighter needs to have excellent written skills. This is evaluated based on your application and your resume. Firefighters are expected to complete daily apparatus and equipment maintenance paperwork, as well as patient care reports (PCR's). Firefighters in smaller departments are also expected to sometimes be in charge of different programs, which may require proposal writing, budget preparation, and other related paperwork.

Reason #11: Poor personal appearance or presentation.

You can be the best at your trade or craft, but if the public perceives you as having a poor personal appearance or presentation, all of your talent will probably go unnoticed. Is it fair? Of course not; is it reality? Of course it is. If you do not take the time or effort to make yourself look professional and presentable during the phases of the hiring process, do not expect a department to take the chance on you risking their positive public image.

Reason #12: Lack of maturity.

Firefighters are expected to act and be mature. We do not care if you are 18 years old or 55 years old; if you are working as a firefighter, you are expected to display maturity around others, including the public. Many candidates fail to realize that they are getting evaluated for maturity during the hiring process, especially during the oral interview. Lack of maturity can come across in the way you dress, the way you act, the way you answer your questions, and the way you make your decisions.

Reason #13: Arrest or conviction record.

Most fire departments will not hire convicted felons, and will be very selective about hiring folks with misdemeanor records. Why? Because they can! It goes back to supply and demand and the concept of "the best predictor of future behavior is past behavior."

Reason #14: Excessive alcohol or drug usage history.

While virtually every fire department has an Employee Assistance Program for its members, do not be the one that feels they have to use up all of the free visits they are entitled to. Many fire departments will not hire candidates with a driving under the influence (DUI) on their record. Most fire departments realize that there is no "perfect candidate" out there and that we have all made some mistakes in our pasts. The key is whether you have learned from your mistakes (many do not and will probably never learn) and how long ago the incidents were. Stopping your drug use a month before the hiring process began will probably not be long enough of duration of non-use to be hired.

There is nothing against having an alcoholic beverage (assuming you are over 21 years old and not operating motor vehicles while doing so); just as long as you can prove that you are a responsible drinker, you are ok. Illegal drugs on the other hand, are a different story. I love it when I hear "didn't everyone try some drugs while they were younger, or in high school?" Not everyone did. If you did some experimentation, then hopefully that was all that it was. Experimentation does not mean usage on a regular or semi-regular basis, over a course of a few years (or more).

The key factor when doing your background investigation is to not hide anything and to not lie. Let me repeat that. The key factor when doing your background investigation is to not hide anything and to not lie. If you did something in the past (something which you had a choice to do or not to do), then own up and be responsible for your actions and accountable for the consequences of your actions. Not being able to do so can and usually will lead to disqualification.

Reason #15: Lack of confidence and poise; nervous; ill at ease.

Firefighters are expected to be outgoing and confident. We are called upon when the systems in place have failed and we typically see people when they are at their worst, or in situations of need, or severe need. You are there to mitigate their emergency and solve their problem the best you can. Being confident in your knowledge, skills, and abilities, in addition to your presentation and presence, can do wonders at calming down the people you are there to assist.

I remember a call when I was a new paramedic. We were called to a house for a teenage female that had kicked the bed, while playing with her sisters. She had kicked the bed so hard, she had given herself an open fracture to her leg. I had never seen an open, angulated fracture in front of my eyes (outside of pictures in medical textbooks and magazines). It was ugly! Well, I did not help the situation when I looked at it and said "oh s—t." I immediately knew it was a stupid thing to say when I saw the girl start crying, her younger sisters start crying, and her parents looking at me like I had no clue about what to do; after of course, they picked up their jaws from the ground. Luckily, my crew did a great job and we overcame what could have been a disastrous public relations event.

That above incident taught me the importance of command presence and of acting like a duck in times of a crisis or high-stress situations – a duck looks calm on top of the water, however their feet are under the water paddling like crazy!

Reason #16: Lack of interest and enthusiasm; passive; indifferent.

Even though you may think you are interested in something, or think that you are showing enthusiasm, this is an area that really separates the great candidates from the not-so-great candidates. Most oral board candidates do not portray much enthusiasm. When an oral board actually finds the rare candidate who is expressing their enthusiasm for the career as well as for the department they are testing for, they have no choice but to smile and internally cheer that person on. We want to work with enthusiastic people who are actually interested in their chosen profession and are actually interested in becoming the best firefighter they can be as well as the best public servant they can be.

Reason #17: Inability to properly provide all of the required information (certificates, transcripts, etc.).

Many candidates fail to read ALL of the information that is provided on a job application. Why? Because I think that is human nature – to not completely read something they are participating in. It happens all the time. Have you ever heard the saying "read the fine print?" That applies to you when you obtain the job application and are completing and filing your application. Many job applications specifically state something like "please include copies of the required certificates (such as EMT, paramedic, CPR, etc.)." Not doing so shows the people reviewing your application that you cannot follow directions and that you are not someone who is thorough or complete when they do something. Firefighters need to follow directions, be thorough, and be complete, every time they do something.

Reason #18: Failure to keep up required certificates or licenses.

In addition to providing documentation when you submit an application, there is also the expectation that you will keep your certificates and licenses current. Remember, if a certificate such as CPR or EMT is expired even one day, then you cannot say that you are currently certified in that discipline. I get at least one phone call a week from someone in desperate need of a CPR class or an EMT refresher class because their certificate is either expired or soon-to-be expired. Typically when they call me, I am not able to offer them assistance because one of our classes has either just ended or will not start again in time for them to stay current.

If you work for a private company (such as a hospital or ambulance company), and you let your EMT certificate or paramedic license expire (both of which are typically conditions of employment – meaning if you do not have current certification or licensure, you are subject to termination, suspension, reduction of pay, or other forms of discipline) do not expect much sympathy from your supervisors for your lack of judgment or lack of planning.

If you work for a public agency (such as a fire department), many places of work have rules and regulations dealing with maintaining current and valid certifications and licenses (such as EMT, paramedic, driver's license, etc.) or risking termination or other forms of discipline.

Most fire departments track the certificates and licenses of their personnel, as well as the expiration dates. Some departments even send out reminder notices (180 days until expiration, 120 days until expiration, 90 days until expiration, etc.) as a courtesy reminder, even though they shouldn't have to take the time to do so since it is each person's responsibility to track their own credentials. Then, if a firefighter or captain lets their EMT certificate or paramedic license expire, even for one day, they may be immediately pulled from duty, reassigned to a non-functioning EMS position, and be subject to progressive discipline, up to and including termination due to the liability of touching patients without a valid credential. Additionally, the local EMS agency may also get involved and impose their own level of progressive discipline.

I've known many candidates lose out on firefighter jobs because of expired certificates. They put down on their application that they had the certificate, but when it came time to produce a copy of the certificate (such as during the background investigation), and they were unable to do so, they were immediately dropped from consideration and not allowed to continue in the hiring process. Moral of the story – plan ahead, take matters into your own hands, be responsible for your own actions, and be on top of your certificates and other time-sensitive items relating to your life!

Reason #19: History of inability to get along well with others.

At the fire station, we live with each other for 24 hours a day. You will spend a third of your life at the fire station (since we work once every three days), and the firefighters you work with will be your second family. Ask many company officers and battalion chiefs what a good portion of their time is spent on, and you will find out that personnel related issues (people not getting along) take up a good amount of their time. Can't we all just get along?

Reason #20: History of making poor judgments and/or decisions.

Everybody makes mistakes. The key is whether you learn from your mistakes and don't make the same mistake twice. Poor judgments and/ or decisions in your past that can eliminate you (or severely reduce your chances of getting hired) include: getting arrested, excessive accidents or tickets, getting fired, anger management or aggressive tendencies issues, poor credit, etc.

Reason #21: Poor track record with your former and/or present employer(s).

As they say, "the best predictor of future behavior is past behavior." Your track record speaks for itself, both in your personal life and your professional life. If you had an absentee or tardiness problem at your former (or present) employer, there is a good chance you will have the same problem at the fire department.

Reason #22: You do not appear that you would fit into "the culture of the organization."

Many people think they have to wow the oral board with their qualifications. That is not true. All you are doing in an oral board, is "auditioning for the family." The oral board members are looking at you to evaluate how well you will fit into the culture of their organization (realize every fire department has a different culture), how well you will get along with the other firefighters, and how trainable you are. Many departments don't really care about how many qualifications you might have as much as how trainable you are.

Reason #23: Failure to follow directions.

Failure to follow directions, especially on the emergency scene, can lead to the serious injury or death of yourself, your co-workers, or the public. In some ways, this ties into number 17 above, inability to properly provide all of the required information (certificates, transcripts, etc.). However, I decided to keep it separate to stress the importance of following directions.

Realize you are getting tested on your ability to follow directions starting with the time you obtain your application and submit your application, and ending with the time you retire! Other examples of how you are tested for following directions include: being able to show up to the proper location of a certain phase of the testing process (written test, oral interview, etc.), being able to show up on time (hopefully early), being able to completely answer the oral interview question you are being asked, and being able to follow the directions of the proctors of the various phases of the testing process.

Reason #24: Poor physical conditioning.

Let's face it, a good majority of the United States population is overweight, and a number of firefighters also fit into that category. Poor physical conditioning is a big reason many candidates either do not get hired or get terminated during the academy or probation. If you are out of shape, how do you expect to take care of yourself, let alone your co-workers during an emergency situation? Heart attacks still remain the number one killer of firefighters.

Reason #25: Last but not least, you failed to make a proper first impression!

Remember that saying "you don't get a second chance to make a first impression!" It is quite true and it will help you get started off on the right foot. Many (if not all) of the above reasons are also grounds for termination during probation. Getting terminated during probation severely decreases your chances at ever getting hired by another fire department in the future.

Items That May Disqualify A Candidate

Many future firefighters ask the question "what could disqualify me during a background investigation or eliminate me from the hiring process?" I wish there was an easy answer, but there is none. One fire department may have slightly (or drastically) different items that would consider a candidate to be ruled ineligible for a position. Some departments keep this information secret, and some as you will see below make the information public. The challenge for the firefighter candidate is that you may not know what will disqualify you in advance of participating in a hiring process for a fire department. While that may seem a waste of your time (assuming you're already thinking the worst case scenario and feel you won't get hired anyway), if you have that negative attitude, you'll never get hired.

I encourage all candidates to go through the hiring process, unless the job flyer specifically provides disqualifying information, as you will see below. If they do provide the information up front and you meet items to disqualify a candidate, then I say it would be a waste of your time to continue. However, if they don't state what will disqualify you, unless you have a felony or something so embarrassing or disgusting in your background, go through the hiring process and see how far you can get. What's the worst that could happen? You could possibly get offered a job! Getting back to what will disqualify a firefighter candidate during a hiring process, there is no easy answer. However, having any of the following items in your past (or in your future while pursuing the career of firefighter) will more than likely increase your chances of NOT getting hired as a firefighter:

- A failure to keep any scheduled appointments with the department or related to the hiring process.
- Any falsifications (false statements) or intentional omission of any information requested of you during the process (such as on your application or background packet or during your oral interview).
- A failure to submit all of the required documentation on time or in the format requested.
- Any history of driver license suspensions or revocations.
- Any history of automobile insurance cancellations or lack of insurance.
- Any history of injected steroids.
- Any history of selling or manufacturing of drugs or narcotics.
- Any illegal drug use in the last two (2) years.
- A history of greater than three (3) moving violations in the past three (3) years.
- Being at fault in three (3) or more traffic violations in the past three (3) years.
- Any history of convictions (felonies and even some misdemeanors).
- Any military discipline such as a court martial or dishonorable discharge.
- A history of inappropriate, illegal, or unethical behavior and/or activity.
- Theft, dishonesty, and any other character issues that may bring discredit to you and/or your employment with the department, in the event you were given an offer of employment.

Remember that nobody is perfect and that every fire department has different requirements and items that can and / or will disqualify you. The reason why I am providing this information to you is because I don't want you to lose the shot at becoming a firefighter. Every person reading this has probably done or possesses one or more of the above reasons. The key is to recognize that these reasons can eliminate you from the process and to work on any weaknesses you may possess so you never find yourself in the same position others have been in!

Here is an example of wording that was found in a recent firefighter job flyer relating to the requirements of a "good driving record:"

Requirements of a good driving record:

(Criteria must be met by the time of appointment to the position):

1. No type "A" conviction during the past thirty-six (36) months and no more than one (1) type "A" conviction during the past sixty (60) months.
2. No more than one (1) type "B" conviction during the past twelve (12) months and no more than two (2) type "B" convictions during the past thirty-six (36) months.

Type "A" Convictions:

- Driving while intoxicated.
- Reckless driving.
- Speed contest.
- Driving while suspended.
- Driving under the influence of drugs or alcohol.
- Hit and run.
- Grand theft auto.
- Driving while in the possession of an open container of an alcohol beverage.
- Aggravated assault with a motor vehicle.
- Negligent homicide arising out of the use of a motor vehicle (gross negligence).
- Using a motor vehicle for commission of a felony.
- Permitting a non-licensed person to drive.

Type "B" Convictions:

- All moving traffic violations that are not listed as type "A" violations above.

Most fire departments will never tell you why you were eliminated from the hiring process, unless it was totally obvious: you didn't score high enough on the written examination, you did not meet the time standard for the physical ability test, you didn't score high enough on the oral interview, etc. Departments will usually not tell you why you failed the background investigation (or probation for that matter) because it then opens them up to liability and lawsuits. With everyone so sue happy these days, you can't blame a department for trying to protect itself. The obvious problem for the candidate that was eliminated from the process was that they will never know why they were not suitable for employment. How can you improve, change, or defend something if you don't even know what it is you're trying to focus on?

Our destiny is provided thanks to the choices we make (good or bad) in life. One dumb mistake or poor choice can cost you a shot at the best career in the world. Turn those negatives into positives and increase your chances of becoming a firefighter!

Personal History Questionnaire

It is not uncommon for a department to have the firefighter candidate complete a Personal History Questionnaire (PHQ) at the time they apply for the position. Why would they do this as opposed to wait for the background investigation? They use it as a screening tool to not waste future time and money on you. It's a great way for a department to weed out undesirable candidates right from the get-go and not waste either party's time or energy. Yes, it may suck getting dropped from the process from the get-go, but isn't that better than getting all the way through the process and then finding out they don't want you after you've put a lot of time and energy into the process?

Sample PHQ:

A thorough background investigation, which may include a polygraph examination, is part of the screening process for our department, to ensure that the firefighters it hires will be successful in performing their required duties. This questionnaire is a part of that process. Please read the questions carefully and answer them as fully and accurately as you can. The information you provide will be checked with other sources and with other employers to whom you have applied for jobs. If it is determined that the information you have supplied is inaccurate or incomplete, you may be disqualified for the subject issue and for dishonesty during the background investigation. This is a serious matter for the Department because honesty is imperative in a firefighter.

1. Do you own and operate a motor vehicle? Yes or No
2. If you own and operate a motor vehicle but do not have vehicle insurance, how long have you been without insurance?
   a. Does not apply – you currently have motor vehicle insurance for the vehicle(s) you own or you do not own and operate a motor vehicle.
   b. Less than 6 months.
   c. For the last 6 months.
   d. For the last 12 months.
   e. For more than 12 months.
3. In the past five years, what is your total number of at-fault traffic accidents and traffic citations for moving violations? (Moving violations include: speeding, illegal U-turns, illegal lane changes, following too close, double parking, helmet law, and carpool violations).
   a. None
   b. 1-2
   c. 3-4
   d. 5 or more
4. Are you delinquent in any payments you owe for credit cards, loans, child/spousal support, utility bills, taxes, or other debts? Yes or No
5. If you have filed for bankruptcy within the past two (2) years, have you re-established credit and/or a payment record of at least twelve (12) months of timely payments on any debts incurred since the filing for bankruptcy?
   a. Does not apply (you have not filed for bankruptcy within the past two years).
   b. Yes
   c. No
6. Does your employment history include any of the following? Mark all boxes that apply; leave blank if no boxes apply.

    a. Terminated from any job or resigned to avoid termination.

    b. History of discipline, unsatisfactory work performance, absenteeism, or tardiness.

    c. No history of achievement through promotion or increased responsibilities.

    d. Numerous short-term, entry-level jobs in a variety of fields.

7. Have you ever been convicted of a misdemeanor offense as a juvenile or as an adult? Yes or No

8. Have you ever been convicted of a felony offense as a juvenile or adult? Yes or No

9. Have you ever been convicted for assault or battery? Yes or No

10. When was the last time you drove while under the influence of alcohol? For the purpose of this question, consider under the influence as when you may have been arrested if stopped by the police.

    a. Never

    b. Within last 6 months

    c. Within last 12 months

    d. More than 12 months ago

11. Have you ever engaged in any of the activities listed below for drugs, narcotics or illegal substances including marijuana? Mark all boxes that apply; leave blank if no boxes apply.

    a. Sold

    b. Furnished

    c. Manufactured

    d. Cultivated

    e. Used

25 Reasons To Hire You As A Firefighter

The process to become a firefighter is very challenging and frustrating. I would venture for every person hired in the fire service, there are at least ten that are not hired in the fire service. The number ten may be small, and in reality, the number is probably much, much higher.

However, that should not deter you from obtaining the career of your dreams. While it will not be an easy process to become a firefighter, it will sure be worth all of the time and effort you put into the journey, once you receive that badge. It took me approximately four and a half years to become a firefighter, and it was time well spent. I could not think of anything else I would want to be doing with my life. For a 30-year career in the fire service, spending a few years trying to become a firefighter is the cost of doing business.

Does luck play a part in getting hired as a firefighter? Of course it does. However, luck is not the primary reason you get a job offer. To get that far in the hiring process, you must have first successfully passed all phases of the hiring process and also shown some promise that you would be a good return on a department's investment.

While this list is not inclusive, it does provide a good starting point of how to properly prepare and market yourself to a fire department that is looking to make a good investment and hire the best personnel to serve their customers. Use this list not only when you are preparing to become a firefighter, but also while you are preparing yourself for each phase of the hiring process (completing the application, taking the written test, taking the oral interview, etc.) and while you are participating in each phase of the hiring process.

Here are 25 reasons to hire you as a firefighter:

1. You have significant formal education (two year, four year degree) in fire technology or a closely related field.
2. You have more than the minimum in the way of Certifications/ Licenses. Having just the minimum allows you to apply for the position. Going above and beyond, and getting the certificates and licenses that are considered highly desirable will help set you apart from the other candidates.
3. You have an extensive, significant and diverse life experience background to offer.
4. You have an extensive, significant and diverse work experience background to offer.
5. You have an extensive, significant and diverse volunteer/ community service background to offer.
6. You have excellent oral communication skills.
7. You have excellent written communication skills.
8. You have an extensive knowledge and understanding of mechanical ability.
9. You have a sparkling, cheery and positive personality.
10. You have a contagious enthusiasm in whatever you are doing or wanting to do.
11. You have an extensive and significant track record of being dependable.
12. You have excellent computer skills.
13. You demonstrate exceptional leadership ability.
14. You demonstrate the ability to get along with others.
15. You have a clean background to offer, in the way of credit history, employment history, arrest record, and character references.
16. You have bilingual ability in any two languages, at least one being English.
17. You are physically fit and are able to demonstrate you lead a relatively healthy lifestyle.

18. You are capable of being a low maintenance employee for your supervisors. Someone that needs little direction or correction.
19. You demonstrate solid decision-making ability.
20. You understand the word integrity, and are able to demonstrate you have it.
21. You are able to demonstrate that you are a hard-worker, and someone that does not mind getting dirty and doing what needs to be done, when it needs to be done.
22. You have sincere and incredible passion for the fire service and for helping and serving others in time of need.
23. You have military background to offer and understand the chain of command and working in a para-military environment.
24. You are a self-starter, and do not rely on others to tell you what needs to be done and when it needs to be done.
25. You demonstrate that you are unique in a positive way. Most firefighter candidates all look the same in regards to preparation, education, looks, etc. Be the one that stands out in a positive and unique way throughout the hiring process and you will rise to the top.

Remember, there is no "one-size-fits-all" formula to use to get hired as a firefighter. What works for one person may not work for another. What works in one fire department may not work in another. It is up to you to find out what works best for you and to stick with that course of action, ensuring that you are doing as many of the abovementioned items as possible to increase your chances for successfully becoming a firefighter. You can have the best resume in the world with the most qualifications, but if you cannot sell yourself, your knowledge, skills, and abilities, as well as your qualities and traits to the oral board, you will never get hired!

How Old Is Too Old To
Become A Firefighter?

Many people ask me, am I too old to become a firefighter? Or, how old is too old to become a firefighter? Those are two questions that do not have easy answers. Years ago, it was not uncommon to see on a job flyer that the maximum age to apply for a firefighter position was 30 or 35 years old. However, it is presently against Federal Law to discriminate against someone for the reasons of sex, religion, disabilities, ethnicity, or age. What does that mean for you, the future firefighter? It means that you still stand a chance to obtain the career of your dreams!

States and local governments have the ability to impose a maximum hiring age for public safety positions for a variety of reasons, which is why you still may see a maximum hiring age of say 35 years old. Are there people over the age of 35 that can do the job? Of course there are. However, since that department has a mandatory retirement age of 55 years old and you couple the fact that a person has to put in at least 20 years of service to be eligible to receive a retirement pension, hiring someone over 35 would not allow them to obtain 20 years.

Take a look at any year's National Fire Protection Association's Firefighter Fatalities report and you will see the rate of on-the-job deaths for firefighters over the age of 50 is typically two thirds higher than the average and 3.5 times higher than the average for firefighters over the age of 50. If a state or local government has a mandatory retirement age or a maximum hiring age, your chances of successfully overturning those age limits are virtually nil.

Do not get discouraged because you perceive yourself to be too young or too old. When I was hired, there was someone in their early 20's and people in their late 30's. In other past hiring processes, it wasn't uncommon for us to hire folks in their early 20's and folks in their mid 40's. Age is what you, the candidate make of it. Because of the Federal Law I mentioned above, many departments do not even ask for your birth date on the initial application. Some departments do not even want to know your date of birth until you are either offered a job or are participating in the background investigation. That way, they cannot discriminate against you based on your age.

As a candidate, I would not mention my age at any point during the hiring process, unless I was specifically asked about it on an application or during the background investigation paperwork process. Some candidates want to mention their age during their opening statement when they are attempting to sell themselves to the oral panel. For example, "good morning everyone, my name is Joe Smith and I am 20 years of age, let me show you how my qualifications have prepared me to become a firefighter."

While this may sound good to you, don't do it! It may work to your advantage, but there is a great chance that it will work against you. But wait you're thinking, I thought they couldn't discriminate against a candidate based on age? They are not supposed to; however, if you state something such as your age (when you were not asked to), then you run the risk of it going against you. Don't take that chance; it isn't worth it.

Remember, even if an oral board or fire department is required to be objective during a hiring process, it doesn't mean that the process will be 100% objective. Why? Because of the human factor – we are all biased in some form or fashion, and it is virtually impossible to remain 100% objective in anything we do (even with laws and training sessions meant to keep us on track). Most oral board panel members are trained to be objective prior to the oral board by some human resources person. However, this doesn't always occur and even if it does occur, it doesn't mean that the preconceived biases, prejudices, and discriminations of the oral board members will be completely eliminated.

Knowing that, why take the risk of getting discriminated against because of age? Remember that every department is different, yet similar. Some departments tend to prefer hiring younger folks that have minimal or no experience so they can train them the way they want to and so they can come with no preconceived notions of firefighting. This helps eliminate the "when I worked for Acme Fire Department, we did it this way" comments that we just love to hear.

Some departments tend to prefer hiring older folks that have some life experience and maybe even some firefighting experience. This helps eliminate the babysitting and handholding that sometimes occurs with the younger folks that have lived at home their whole lives and had their parents wait on them hand and foot. Additionally, some departments prefer hiring older folks because they will probably stay with that department for their entire career, and also appreciate the job more because they have already had the opportunity to bust their rear at a real job.

And then there are most departments that do not really care about the age of the candidates they hire. I have heard of some departments that have had recruits in the academy as young as 18 years old and as seasoned as 50 years old. That proves that age doesn't matter. What does matter is that you are able to pass ALL of the phases of the hiring process and successfully transition yourself into the fire department that takes a chance on you to become a productive and capable member of the fire service.

Do You Really Know What You're Getting Into?

If it is because of Rescue Me, Chicago Fire, Ladder 49, Backdraft (or any other television show or movie), you may be in for a surprise!

I would venture many future firefighters and some current firefighters were inspired to get into the career because of watching television shows or movies that focused on the fire service. Now while there is not necessarily anything wrong with that, I hope you realize that what goes on a television show or movie is typically not the same way that things occur in real life. For example, how many times have you seen a car on fire explode on television or in a movie? Almost every time there is a fire. I have yet to see a vehicle fire that had the fuel tank explode (not to say it won't happen); I have seen tires and air struts explode, but that is not the whole vehicle.

Or, how many times have you seen a fire sprinkler system activate during a building fire on television or a movie and all of the heads simultaneously activate, drenching the entire room? Regarding fire sprinklers, once you have had some training and education on this subject, you'll realize that most often (unless it is a deluge system where all sprinkler heads activate, such as found in a high value area, and not that common), one sprinkler head will contain the fire.

Or, how many fires have you seen on television or the movies that have the building engulfed in flames (fully involved as we call it), but there is perfect visibility in the room? On virtually every structure fire

I have ever been to where the structure was on fire (even in one room, a "room and contents fire" as we call them), we have always been greeted by smoke banked from the ceiling down to the floor, forcing us to drop to our knees and crawl through the house, with the hose, searching for any victims and for the seat of the fire to start getting water on it. The list goes on.

What do these two examples do in terms of public perception? Not much; the public typically believes what they want to believe, based on television, movies, or their real-life experiences (which typically do not involve 9-1-1 calls for service).

The point I'm trying to make is that the way Hollywood portrays us in not the same life style or environment that a typical firefighter experiences. Hollywood does what it does to make money, provide entertainment, and bring in customers. The average firefighter does not experience fires every shift and getting the opportunity to save someone from the clutches of death on an everyday basis either.

This can work for us or against us in the eyes of the public, especially our family and friends that are watching these shows and starting to put an image into their brain of what a firefighter does. Your job, if you accept it, is to start educating yourself on the fire service through formal education and research and start explaining the differences to them. What a Firefighter in New York City (especially the Bronx) is going to experience over 10 years is significantly different than what a Firefighter in Piedmont, California is going to experience over 30 years.

This is not meant to say one Firefighter is better than the other, based on where they work. It is what it is; a Firefighter working for a big city fire department is going to see more action and gain more experience in a shorter amount of time than a Firefighter would working in a community with virtually no commercial occupancies, very expensive homes with sprinklers and other fire protection devices, and highly educated people that typically do not use the 9-1-1 system. I know some Firefighters within the Piedmont Fire Department, and I have nothing but the utmost respect for them and what they do.

My point is that where you work will dictate what you are exposed to. Working in a busy big city fire department will definitely increase your chances of getting injured, exposed to a communicable disease or health hazard, or even killed, as opposed to working in a wealthier community that does not respond to as many calls. However, don't let your guard down – firefighters get killed in every size and shape fire department, and working in a small, suburban department can also be tragic because of the lower call and fire volume. People tend to let their guard down and think "firefighters only get killed in the big city." I've heard it, especially in my department. Then, when we lost my good friend Captain Mark McCormack in the course of fighting a structure fire on February 13, 2005, we realized, yes, it can happen here.

Odds are a firefighter will be killed in the line of duty in every fire department; the key is whether it is in the near future or 500 years from now. I don't say that negatively or pessimistically, I just say that to reinforce to you to not let your guard down and always be highly trained and looking to continue your education and experience in any possible way you can, regardless of what size department you may end up working for.

Understanding Fire Service
Wages & Benefits

Becoming a firefighter to make you rich is not probably the best idea. If you want to make lots of money, do not go to work for the public sector, find a career in the private sector. Don't get me wrong, most of us are paid well for what we do, but there are many firefighters that are not and have to take on second jobs or work every ounce of overtime just to make ends meet. Granted, some of those firefighters could probably survive better if they had a spouse / partner that had a job or they did not have such a special affinity for what I call "firefighter toys," – not just having one vehicle, but having a second or third vehicle, a motorcycle, a jet ski, an all-terrain vehicle (ATV), a boat, etc.

Many firefighters across the nation cannot afford to live in the areas they protect (me being one of them). My salary alone would barely qualify for a condominium in the majority of the areas protected by my department. A two-income household is required to live in the majority of our areas protected, and that will typically only buy a three-bedroom fixer upper house, of which there is a minimal supply. Most personnel (myself included) have been forced to find homes outside of the fire department's jurisdictional boundaries, something I do not like.

I wish I lived in the same community I protected for many reasons: to be able to have my tax dollars go back into our department in some form or fashion, to be able to have a better understanding and loyalty to my community, and to have a better knowledge of the area and the buildings to use in times of emergency. Regardless, I found a home a couple of blocks outside of our area in the next city over that was a little more affordable. Close enough, yet not too far away. Many firefighters choose to not live in the communities they are employed by (when they have the ability to afford a house in the same community), and that is their right to do so.

When looking at a job flyer for a firefighter position, you will typically see the salary listed as either the yearly salary or the monthly salary. Not every department lists the salary range the same way. Some salaries include add-on bonuses (such as for EMT certification, educational accomplishments, etc.) as well as retirement or healthcare contributions. Don't get too excited when you see a high salary (as opposed to what you have normally seen for a firefighter). On the same token, don't get down and not take a department's test just because of a perceived low salary. That low salary might be shown without any add-on bonuses (commonly called incentive pay). The moral of the story? When comparing fire department salaries, try to compare apples with apples. Understand the wording of the job flyer and what to look for when comparing salaries.

Two examples of a typical firefighter salary schedule:

Example #1:

Salary:

The monthly salary range is $3973 to $6469. (The top step includes the EMT bonus). In addition, the City pays 5.5% of the employee's contribution to the Public Employees' Retirement System and the employee pays 3.5%.

Example #2:

Salary:

$4,055 - $4,257 - $4,470 - $4,694 - $4,928 per month. In addition to the stated salary, the City pays the employee's 9% share of the Public Employees Retirement System contribution for 3 @ 55 and provides each employee with a monthly health insurance allowance of $955.41 of which the unused remainder is returned to the employee.

The only difference (besides actual salary) between example 1 and 2 is that example 2 spells out the five separate "step raises" a firefighter will receive, where example 1 just lists the range. Even though example 1 does not show how many "steps" there are to go from the lowest to the highest salary, it is probably safe to say there are usually five to seven steps, and each step usually takes one year of service to get to the next step.

So, for example #2, a person hired on January 1, will start out at $4,055 per month. Then, on January 1, the following year (assuming they successfully pass the one-year probationary period), they will reach step 2 and then start receiving $4,257 per month. Then on January 1, the third year on the job, they will reach step 3 at $4,470 per month. This will continue until the fifth year of employment where they reach the "top step" of $4,928. At that point, the only other raises they will receive for the rest of their career will usually only be from cost-of-living increases or other forms of increased compensation that is received after their labor organization successfully negotiates their current labor/management agreement. If someone promotes to a higher rank, they will also typically have to start out and go through the next set of step raises of that higher rank. So, if a firefighter with eight years on the job (already at top step firefighter since it took four years to reach top step) is promoted to captain, they may go from top step firefighter to step 1 captain – and then start the cycle again at their new rank, getting a step raise once a year until they reach top stop.

Key Points About Fire Service Salaries:

- Overtime is not a right; it is a privilege. Many firefighters live their lives and budget things based on overtime. This is extremely risky, especially in tough economic times because it is quite possible the overtime may stop, or be dramatically reduced.

- Fire service salaries are public information; it is quite possible that you may see your name, tied into your salary and even how much overtime and/or total compensation you received in the newspaper or on the nightly news. The news media has the right to do this, so there is no reason to get emotional or angry since that information is public information. Instead, channel your negative energy to positive energy and do what it takes to prove you are every bit worth the money you are being paid.

So, You Want To Become a Firefighter? 5 Guidelines to Assist You

Becoming a firefighter is not easy. If it were easy, everyone would be doing it. It takes a great deal of perseverance, patience, persistence, dedication and good old-fashioned hard work to become a firefighter. Nothing in life comes easy; especially when you want to have one of the best careers a person could ever dream to have.

How long will it take to become a firefighter? That question cannot easily be answered because it really comes down to "what you give is what you get." Not every person that starts out to become a firefighter ends up becoming a firefighter. For that matter, not every person that ever goes to medical school becomes a doctor; not every person that ever goes to law school ever becomes a lawyer.

I cannot guarantee that you will ever reach your dream of becoming a firefighter. What I can guarantee you is that if you never give up on obtaining your dream of becoming a firefighter, then your odds of succeeding greatly increase. On the average, I would say it takes anywhere from three (3) to seven (7) years to become a full-time paid firefighter. Some do it in less time, some do it in more time, and some never get the chance to do it at all. I have known people to take 10 to 15 years to become a firefighter. I have known people to give up after a year of trying to become a firefighter.

What's the moral of the story? If you give up, you give up your dream. If you continue pursuing your dream and continue doing whatever it takes to achieve that dream, continuously working on improving your weaknesses, keeping up your strengths, and preparing yourself to be the best candidate that you can be, then you stand the chance of actually achieving that dream!

Beginning the process:

Once you have determined that it is your dream to become a firefighter, then it is time to put your money where your mouth is and start preparing yourself on a full-time basis. It is a full-time job just getting the job!

Here are five basic steps to assist you in becoming a firefighter:

Step 1: Enroll as a student at a community college offering a two-year degree in Fire Technology or Fire Science.

This can be done in person at the college or via their website.

Step 2: Begin taking classes to work towards your two-year degree in Fire Technology.

My suggested course of action for you is as follows. *Note, the classes listed are what are offered at Chabot College in Hayward, California, where I teach. The classes at other colleges may slightly differ.*

First semester:

- **Health 61** (EMS First Responder – the prerequisite to get into our EMT program)
- **Kinesiology 20** (Fire conditioning)
- **Fire 50** (Introduction to Fire Protection Organization – a prerequisite for the firefighter 1 academy)
- **Fire 52** (Firefighter Safety and Public Education - a prerequisite for the firefighter 1 academy)
- **Fire 53** (Fire Behavior and Combustion)
- **Sign up for and successfully pass the Candidate Physical**

Ability Test (CPAT). For more information on the CPAT, go to http://www.cpatonline.org - since more and more departments are requiring a person to possess a current (no older than 1 year) CPAT completion certificate.

- **Take any general education units towards your degree** (for specific general education units, talk to a college counselor)
- **Start building up volunteer experience** (anything you volunteer your time for is highly looked upon by fire departments, and it doesn't necessarily have to be fire or EMS related).
- **Start learning as much as you can about the fire service and the job of a firefighter.** Visit your local fire stations and start talking with the firefighters to build contacts and learn more about firefighting as a career. Also, start visiting fire department websites to see how each fire department is unique and what they have to offer.
- **Start taking every firefighter examination you qualify for** (see step #3 below for more information). Yes, you may qualify for some that only require you to be 18 years old and have a high school diploma or G.E.D. Start learning about the firefighter hiring process by taking the tests.

Second semester:

- **Health 81** (EMT training course).
- **Fire 51** (Fire Service Operations - a prerequisite for the firefighter 1 academy).
- **Fire 54** (Fire Prevention Technology).
- **Fire 56** (Building Construction for Fire Protection).
- **Fire 89** (Firefighter 1 Academy Introduction).
- **Take any general education units towards your degree** (for specific general education units, talk to a college counselor).

Third semester:

- **Fire 90A, 90B, 90C** (Firefighter 1 Academy).

- **Fire 91A** (Wildland firefighting).
- **Fire 91B** (Haz Mat first responder - Operations).
- **Fire 91C** (I-200; basic ICS).
- **Fire 91D** (Firefighter Survival).
- **Start looking for a job as an EMT with an ambulance company to gain experience and to help you prepare for paramedic school and a career in the fire service** (since Emergency Medical Service responses make up 70% or more of our call volume).

Fourth semester:

- **Fire 55** (Fire Protection Equipment and Systems).
- **Fire 95 and 96** (Fire Department work experience, which you can enroll in for up to 4 semesters, gaining valuable experience for your resume as a student firefighter).
- **Any general education units towards your degree** (for specific general education units, talk to a college counselor).
- **Start looking at getting into a paramedic program.**

NOTE: The exact order may vary slightly, based on your ability to successful enroll and pass the classes. Not every class may be offered every semester. Some students are able to handle the above course load per semester, some can handle more classes per semester, some can handle fewer classes per semester. Also, the above classes reflect the two-year degree in Fire Technology at Chabot College; some other colleges may have a slightly different program.

Do you already have a two year or four year degree in a non-fire discipline?

Many people ask me when they are starting out why they have to get a fire technology two-year degree when they already have a degree in another discipline. Some think it is a waste of time, some think they know what they need to know, some do not have the time to go through more college; some just do not provide a good answer. While the fire service is looking for educated personnel, we are also looking for personnel who have shown a commitment to the fire service. One way to show your commitment to the fire service is by obtaining a two-year degree in fire technology, which should include EMT training, academy training, and education and training in the basics of becoming a firefighter and preparing for future promotional opportunities.

If you have a degree already, here is my suggestion: take your transcripts down to a counselor to see which general education units will transfer over to the college you are applying to be a fire technology student at. Most of your general education should transfer in; I did this when I started out at Chabot College in the early 1990's, after having received my four-year degree. I went to a counselor, and they accepted all but six units of my general education. So, to get a two-year degree in fire technology at Chabot College (as opposed to just a Certificate of Achievement, or no piece of paper whatsoever), all I needed to do was take two, three unit general education classes. That was a no-brainer, and it showed my commitment to the fire service.

Also, imagine not having a fire technology degree when you are in the oral interview, and the oral board asks you "you have a four year degree in Sociology, great, now, tell us how that applies to the fire service?" While I think you can relate a degree in any discipline to the fire service, I think it is tough to really convince the oral board that the fire service is your career choice when you have no formal education in fire technology and you are expecting us to take a chance on someone who has not shown a commitment to the fire service. I would rather take a chance on hiring someone who has completed a two-year degree fire technology program at a community college, including a firefighter 1 academy. I want a proven commodity, so to speak.

Step 3: Start taking as many firefighter entrance examinations as you qualify for.

Every city that has a fire department usually has their own testing process that occurs once every two to four years. For example, if you want to work for the Oakland Fire Department, then you will have to participate in their firefighter examination process.

Some of the requirements to be able to file an application at various fire departments can include:

- Minimum age of 18 or 21 years old.
- Valid driver's license.
- Current EMT certificate.
- Current Paramedic license.
- Firefighter 1 Academy completion.
- Firefighter 1 State certification.
- Current CPR certification.

Some departments require one or more of the above qualifications. It is feasible that you may qualify to take a firefighter entrance exam even before you start taking classes at Chabot College. Is it realistic to get hired as a firefighter without any training or education? No, while it is not realistic, it is not impossible. However, remember that having the above qualifications only allow you to participate in the hiring process; they do not guarantee your success.

You may wonder, why should I get some of the above qualifications if they are not required by the department I am testing for, or why should I get those qualifications (such as a Firefighter 1 certificate or paramedic license) if the department that hires me will put me through that training anyway? Well, first of all, not every department will put you through that training. Plus, that training will allow you to look more attractive or at least equal when compared to your competition (many of whom will look very attractive, at least on paper).

Why go through an academy at a college before getting hired, since most departments will put you through their own academy? For two primary reasons:

1. Think of going through a college fire technology two year degree program and firefighter academy as being similar to a baseball player going through the minor league baseball system,

preparing themselves to be a professional baseball player. How many professional ball players do you know that go straight from high school to pro baseball? Very few. And of those very few, how many have successful careers lasting more than ten years? Even fewer. Most successful professional baseball players have "honed" their skills by playing minor league and college baseball. Think of a two year fire technology program at a community college like minor league baseball. I don't know about you, but I would rather make my mistakes at the college level, not during my probationary period at the fire department (which can lead to termination).

2. When you get hired, it will make that recruit academy they are paying you to go through easier, since most college firefighter 1 academies are more challenging and demanding than many paid fire department academies. Having been through a college academy and degree program will make your paid academy go much smoother since you're just refreshing or relearning concepts or skills you should have learned at the college level. Much less stressful than trying to learn something new once you get hired and then have to maintain an 80% average on your daily quizzes during the academy to keep from getting terminated. Additionally, passing a college firefighter 1 academy tells a department that you are trainable and have the basic skills to enter and hopefully pass the academy.

Other qualifications some fire departments list as "highly desirable" include:

- Bilingual ability in any language.
- Volunteer or paid firefighter experience.
- Volunteer/community service experience in areas other than fire or EMS.
- Fire Technology courses completed from a community college (such as Chabot).
- Additional training certifications such as:

- ○ Rescue Systems 1.
- ○ Hazardous Materials Technician / Specialist.
- ○ Class B Firefighter's restricted driver's license.
- ○ Anything that may be location specific; for example if you are testing for a department has large numbers of waterways, they may require a person to be able to swim, or to have certain training such as Swift Water Rescue Awareness.

KEY POINT: You can have the best resume in the world (meaning you are very qualified on paper), but it will not guarantee you a career as a firefighter. *YOU STILL HAVE TO SELL YOURSELF AND YOUR QUALIFICATIONS TO THE ORAL BOARD DURING THE ORAL INTERVIEW!*

It is up to you to score highly in all phases of the hiring process, which can include (but are not limited to) the following events:

- **Application filing** (submitting your completed application and resume by the filing deadline).
- **Application Screening** (to ensure candidates meet the minimum qualifications and to sometimes select only the most qualified candidates).
- **Written Examination** (usually a 100 question multiple choice test of various subject areas such as math, English, problem solving ability, mechanical aptitude, reading comprehension, ability to follow directions, etc.).
- **Physical Ability Test** (consisting of various events to ensure you meet the minimum physical performance requirements).
- **Oral Interview** (usually making up 100% of your overall ranking on the hiring list. Used to evaluate such areas as oral communications, ethics, problem solving ability, decision making skills, maturity, and ability to get along well with others).
- **Chief's Interview** (a second level interview for those candidates selected to continue in the process. Usually with the fire chief or some other high-ranking chief officers. This interview is usually

designed to get to know you better and find out more regarding your suitability to work for that department).

- **Background Investigation** (designed to do a full investigation on areas such as your educational history, work experience history, credit history, driving record, personal characteristics and attributes, etc.).

- **Psychological Examination** (designed to determine your suitability as a firefighter based on psychological questions).

- **Medical Examination** (designed to determine your fitness for duty through the means of a full body examination and medical screening).

- **Recruit Academy** (if you're lucky enough to successfully pass all of the above phases, then you are usually eligible to receive a job offer and appointment to a recruit academy lasting anywhere from 8 weeks to 20 weeks. This recruit academy sponsored by the hiring department will provide you with firefighting knowledge, skills, and abilities from A to Z).

- **Probation Period** (successfully completing the academy allows you to start working as a probationary firefighter. Probation periods last anywhere from one year to three years. This period is designed to determine if you are suitable for permanent employment).

How do I find out which fire departments are accepting applications and what are the requirements to become a firefighter with that department?

- Subscribe to firefighter examination notification services such as Perfect Firefighter Candidate - http://www.firecareers.com or Careers in the Fire Service - http://www.firerecruit.com - both services are worth every penny of their price. They save you the time and effort of calling each fire department and asking when they are next hiring. Both of these services provide websites with notifications of when departments nationwide are accepting applications.

- Contact individual fire departments and their respective city (or county) personnel (or human resource) offices. To find out how to contact them you can do an Internet search. Typically the personnel department (or human resource department) for a jurisdiction handles the testing process for positions within the fire department. Ask them when they will next be testing for the position of firefighter, what their qualifications are to become a firefighter, do they accept interest cards (if so, can you leave your name with them so you can be notified of their next exam?), and any other relevant questions you may come up with.

Step 4: Begin preparing NOW for your background investigation. This means the following:

- **Maintaining a clean credit and financial history.** Take the time to obtain a credit report on yourself from one of the major companies. Doing this will allow you to see (in advance) what your credit history looks like, prior to the background investigator seeing it. If you have outstanding debt, start composing a plan to eliminate that debt. Close any credit cards you are not utilizing. Pay your bills on time!
- **Maintaining a clean driving record.** Many candidates have been eliminated during the background investigation for excessive accidents (regardless of who was at fault), and excessive traffic related citations (speeding tickets, moving violations, etc.).
- **Maintaining a clean law enforcement record.** What this means is don't get arrested, drive while you are under the influence of alcohol, take any illegal drugs, or do something otherwise stupid you're going to regret for the rest of your life. Think twice before getting into a fight or driving home after having some alcoholic drinks. Performing (and getting caught) any of the above items can virtually eliminate your chances of getting hired as a firefighter.
- **Maintaining an up-to-date list of relatives and friends.**

During a background investigation, you are going to be asked to provide names, addresses and phone numbers of your relatives and close friends so that they can be contacted to vouch for your character and background information you have documented.

- **Maintaining an up-to-date list of your employment history.** Typically, you are going to be asked to provide information from each employer you have worked for over that past 10 years. Some departments require you to provide information from EVERY job you have ever held! Some of the information to obtain now includes name, address and phone number of employer, exact dates employed, exact title(s) you held, exact salaries you were paid, duties and responsibilities, and name of your supervisor.

- **Maintaining an up-to-date list of your educational history.** Typically you are going to be asked to provide information from every educational institution you have attended (after and including high school). Information requested can include name and address of the school, number of units completed, degrees obtained, etc.

Step 5: Other relevant information to assist you in becoming a firefighter:

- Think twice about getting that visible tattoo or getting your body pierced in visible areas. Some fire departments have rules that prohibit visible tattoos or body piercings.

- If you presently smoke, attempt to quit. Many fire departments require you to sign a document stating you have not smoked for the past year, and that you will not smoke at any point while their department employs you.

- Buy yourself one nice outfit to wear to the oral interviews. This includes a nice suit (pants and coat), dress shirt, tie, polished dress shoes, dark socks, etc. Basically a conservative look. Keep the jewelry to a minimum. For females, a nice pantsuit or professional looking dress (not something you would wear out on a date or to a cocktail party). Besides firefighter oral interviews, you can use that suit for weddings, funerals, and other important events. Invest in your wardrobe and it will pay dividends.

- Keep yourself appropriately groomed. Many fire departments have rules prohibiting facial hair (except for a moustache). While some of you might enjoy wearing that goatee or beard, realize you'll have to shave it once you get hired. Get used to not having it now. Wearing a goatee, beard, or even long hair to an interview or during any phase of the hiring process, can severely reduce your chances for getting hired with that department.

NOTE: You might be wondering why I included the above information regarding grooming and personal attributes. While it is a true a fire department is not legally allowed to discriminate based on appearance (among other things), realize that perception is reality. That means that you can be the best paramedic in the world, but if you have tattoos and body piercings all over your body, you're potentially going to be perceived negatively. I'm not saying that's right or wrong; I'm just saying it is human nature and reality.

Avoid the whole situation entirely and just be conservative in your approach. Remember that it is important to stick out in the hiring process; and that means in a positive way, not a negative way! Stick out in a positive way such as having a unique background of experience or other qualifications to bring to the table such as being bilingual or having your paramedic license.

- Start educating yourself on the job of a firefighter and the operations of a fire department so that when you are talking to firefighters, visiting fire stations, and participating in the various events of the hiring process (such as the oral interview), you can talk in an educated way and actually sound like you know what you're talking about. Knowing the difference between an Engine and a Truck is important PRIOR to the oral interview. One way to learn as much as you can about the job of a firefighter and how the operations of fire departments can be similar yet different, start visiting websites of fire departments.

- Start keeping yourself up-to-date on what is going on in the fire service. Have your fingers on the pulse of the fire service by subscribing to the numerous free email mailing lists that provide valuable information such as fire service news stories, employment opportunities, volunteer opportunities, training opportunities and other relevant fire service information to help best prepare you to become a firefighter.

Remember that nothing worth having in life is going to come to you easily. It is up to you to remain positive, remain focused, and remain motivated to continue doing what it takes to become a firefighter.

There are going to be many frustrating and disappointing moments while testing to become a firefighter; the key point is that you recognize your weaknesses, be open to constructive criticism, and continue to pursue that dream of becoming a firefighter. Once you give up, you give up and let someone else take your spot riding on that fire engine you dreamed of riding on!

Becoming An Explorer Firefighter
To Gain Valuable Experience

For those individuals who are not of the age to become a volunteer or paid firefighter (minimum of 18 years old in most departments), one avenue to consider is that of an Explorer Firefighter. Some fire departments and even ambulance companies have established an Explorer Program that is an extension of the Boy Scouts of America, and is usually open to those between the ages of 14 and 18.

Many firefighters like me started out as Explorers. While I was over the age of 18, I was able to become an Associate Advisor for the City of Alameda's Fire Explorer Post 689. This enabled me to not only have fire service experience for my resume, but to also practice the skills I learned in the Chabot College Firefighter 1 Academy since it is not uncommon for graduates to forget the majority of what they learned in an Academy if they don't get the chance to regularly practice those skills.

Not every fire department has an Explorer Post, but if you can find one, and if you are of the appropriate age, it is a great way to get your foot in the door and get some experience on your resume. As an Explorer, don't expect to "fight fire" and be in the thick of the action. Most Explorers are simply observers, due to the amount of liability involved. However, don't let that discourage you; it's experience, better than nothing.

Since Explorers are still typically in middle or high school (based on their age), the requirements to continue to be an Explorer are usually pretty minimal. There may be weekly or monthly meetings or drill sessions to attend at night or on weekends. The cost is usually minimal too; about $8.00 for the Boy Scouts of America fee, maybe a small fee to cover incidental expenses, and then the cost of a basic uniform (Explorer T-Shirt, Ben Davis or Dickies pants, black shoes, etc.).

Becoming an Explorer may lead you to other opportunities if you play your cards right. Just like being a Volunteer Firefighter, being an Explorer Firefighter gives you a 50/50 chance at succeeding in that department. Why? Because now we get to know you; we get to know the REAL you. I say that because many candidates think becoming an Explorer or Volunteer gives them a guaranteed spot once a full-time position opens up. Well, the good part about being an Explorer or a Volunteer is that we get to know you. The bad part is that we get to know you. Meaning if you are someone we want to have work for us and whom we think will fit into our culture, great. But, if we don't like what we've seen you do as an Explorer or Volunteer, you've just shot yourself in the foot.

Remember, the best predictor of future behavior....is past behavior!

Becoming A Volunteer Firefighter
To Gain Valuable Experience

For those of you that have been thinking about taking a volunteer/reserve/auxiliary firefighter test with the hopes of getting experience and exposure to help get you a full-time firefighter position, PLEASE READ THIS INFORMATION CAREFULLY - You just may benefit from it!

A while ago, I had the pleasure of coordinating our volunteer/reserve firefighter testing process. We were looking at picking up 12 people out of about 200 plus applicants. Good odds you might say to yourself - even better once you hear what I have to say. Our department typically picks up about 10 to 15 volunteer firefighters every couple of years. Today, it is not uncommon to get upwards of 500 applicants for 10 to 15 volunteer positions. Why? Because everyone wants to do it and everyone thinks it's an easy way to get a foot in the door.

We have a maximum number of 40 spots to support our almost 300 paid personnel. Our volunteers are mostly support personnel at the scene; they respond to the scene and then meet up with the Incident Commander (IC) to get an assignment. They do not drive apparatus, although they are expected to do ride a longs, make a certain percentage of responses (first alarm or greater incidents), and make a certain percentage of training sessions.

Out of about 200 or so applications filed at the time, we accepted about 150 or so to continue. The ones that got round-filed did so because of not meeting geographical requirements for the most part.

Those 150 or so accepted applications then proceeded to the next phase - the Physical Ability Test (PAT). Of those 150 or so, only about 80 successfully made it through the PAT. Some were no shows, some didn't make the time standard, some couldn't even finish and a couple got transported (yes, transported by ambulance). Those 80 or so then went to the oral interviews.

Here is where I want to make some comments - specifically about our PAT and the almost 50% failure rate. Many of our volunteers and paid personnel were asking why so many didn't pass. Did the time change? No. Did the events change? No. This was the same test I took and most of them took, especially if they were hired within the last 12 or so years. But why the failures? Why the transports? Here are my thoughts to learn from:

1. First of all, this was the FIRST firefighter test for many people. I truly don't think they knew what they were getting into. I bet they do now.
2. Second, studies have shown that a good number of the US population is overweight (more so than the past, or so they say). I asked many that failed if they were in shape or had worked out for such an event and the answer was no.
3. Third, many candidates did not take the process as serious as they would have had it been a full-time firefighter position. Remember - the law, the NFPA, and most importantly fire, do not discriminate between paid and volunteer positions. All firefighters are required and expected to do the same duties and be held to the same standards (whether they are or not is a different story).
4. Fourth - many candidates ate too much prior to the PAT, did not properly hydrate before the PAT, or did not properly eat the night before.
5. Fifth - some candidates arrived late. Oops. The letter we sent out said to arrive at least 30 minutes prior so that they can register. One candidate showed up at 8:05, 35 minutes after he was supposed to be there. I tactfully told him that he would not be

able to continue because he did not follow directions and it is paramount that firefighters follow directions. I made sure I was tactful and respectful and he actually seemed to take it pretty well. Another candidate showed up 45 minutes late, giving the excuse that he was on the wrong street. Once again, I gave him the polite "thanks, but no thanks speech" and advised him he could have prevented this by leaving plenty of time to arrive (expect traffic, car problems, etc.) and if he had driven to the location at least a day prior so that he would have known where to go.

6. Sixth - not following directions. Our letter said to NOT park on the training tower grounds and to park on the city streets. Imagine the look on my face when I see a candidate parking his car on the back apron of the station, right where the engine would have to drive through to get back into the station. I walked up to him and asked him if I could help him. He said yes, he's here for his test. I asked him what time his test was. He said 10 minutes ago (strike one). I then asked if he had read the letter. No (strike two). I then asked him why he parked his car where he did. He said, "what's the big deal." (strike three - thank you for playing, Johnny tell him what he could have won....). You're outta here!

NOTE: For those that didn't get the above reference in #6, I was referring to the Johnny Carson Tonight Show on NBC (Jay Leno took over a number of years ago, and now Jimmy Fallon is set to take over) where Johnny's master of ceremonies Ed McMahon used to say "thank you for playing, Johnny tell him what he could have won" when someone didn't correctly answer the question and basically lost the prize at hand.

Regarding the volunteer firefighter oral interview process let me comment on the ones last time that shined:

1. Treated it like a real full-time FF interview (wore a suit - many did not).

2. Had actually researched the position they were aspiring to (you'd be surprised how many did NOT know what the duties or expectations of the position were). Remember that you will probably be asked questions that can expand (or contract) on that knowledge.

3. Had actually researched the department they aspired to work for (paid or volunteer).

4. Had arrived on time, well in advance.

5. Had treated everyone, including the administrative staff that checked them in, with respect, warmth, sincerity, and enthusiasm.

6. Had actually prepared for the questions they might receive (volunteer questions are typically not any different than paid questions).

7. Had actually taken tests before (this was probably not their first test). How do you find out your weaknesses relating to testing unless you start testing? Don't hold back until your dream department tests to start testing and expect to do good enough to get hired. Think of it this way - how many high school ball players go straight to the major leagues? Very few. And of those very few, how many are success stories or hall of famers? Even fewer. The best ball players have taken the time to hone their craft, practice their part, and learned how to "play the game." Yes, it is a game - whether you believe it or not. Those that learn how to play the game might not be the best firefighters in the eyes of their competition, but they were the best in the eyes of the oral panel or the department they were testing for.

That's about all I can think of. What is the moral of the story? Treat EVERY interview and phase of the volunteer / reserve / auxiliary / cadet hiring process as you would a full-time paid position. Also, remember that good, bad or indifferent - this is a weeding out process.

This is not "t-ball" where everybody gets to play. Just because you want to be a firefighters doesn't mean you'll ever be able to pass all phases of the process or ever be successful. The more you set yourself up for success in advance, the better you will be in the future.

Emergency Medical Service (EMS) Related Volunteer Experience

Besides trying to become a volunteer firefighter, another valuable way to gain relevant volunteer experience is to find ways to practice and hone your EMS skills. Many organizations, such as the American Red Cross, local high schools or colleges, or churches are always on the lookout for people to volunteer their time at EMS related events. At the bare minimum, they typically want someone who is certified to at least the basic CPR level, and the Advanced First Aid level. Don't think you need to be an EMT or a paramedic to volunteer; there are many different roles you can fill to gain valuable EMS experience. Since EMS responses make up 60 to 80% of most fire department's responses, it is critical to have top-notch EMS skills to offer a department.

Also, if you are eventually looking at attending paramedic school (some fire departments only hire certified or licensed paramedics), it is paramount to have EMS experience. If you are having trouble getting hired on an ambulance company as an EMT or paramedic (something I recommend all future firefighters do), then getting volunteer EMS experience may be your foot in the door to get some type of related experience on your resume.

Other Volunteer / Community Service Opportunities

The terms volunteer experience and community service are typically synonymous with each other. Do not think you must have fire or EMS related volunteer experience to successfully get hired as a firefighter. Many candidates get hired every day without having volunteered for a fire department or ambulance company. While this specific experience is very beneficial, not everyone is fortunate enough to have a local fire department or ambulance company looking to pick you up as a volunteer.

Even if you do have fire or EMS related volunteer experience, I also encourage you to get non-fire or non-EMS related volunteer experience. Why? Because doing so helps make you stick out in a unique way. It is not uncommon to find many candidates applying for a position at a fire department all having fire or EMS related volunteer experience. After the first few candidates, they all tend to look the same. Not that this is a bad thing, but the oral board is looking for unique candidates that may bring a different perspective to the fire service. One way to bring a different perspective is to have non-fire or non-EMS related volunteer experience to offer.

There are many non-fire or non-EMS related ways to volunteer your time. Examples can include, but are not limited to: homeless shelters, soup kitchens, local churches, your local city or county governmental center (recreational or activity programs for youths or seniors), your local public or private school (pre-school, elementary, middle, high, or even college), local or national organizations or associations that cater to people in need, cleaning up your community, and anything else you can think of that does not pay you or provide you with any benefits.

Why is volunteer work or community service so important you may wonder? Many fire departments will ask a question during the oral interview and even the chief's interview (second-level interview of a select few candidates being strongly considered for employment) to the effect of: "what type of volunteer or community service work do you currently perform?" Not having an answer to that question will doom your chances of getting hired; you either have an answer or you don't have an answer. Smart and successful firefighter candidates have already prepared for that oral interview question by volunteering their time.

Educating Yourself On The Fire Service Is Paramount To Your Success!

In preceding sections, I have touched on the need to do fire station visits, to stay in tune with current fire service issues by subscribing to fire service trade magazines and fire service email lists, etc., but I want to now focus on why it is so important to do so. Many people want to become firefighters but they have no clue of what they are getting into. They get into the career because of the "10 days a month work schedule," or "to fight fire and save lives," or for the "wages and benefits." They figure they can get a relatively guaranteed career for the next 30 years, earn a decent wage, get a great retirement, and only have to work 10 days a month. Well, if you're getting into the fire service for primarily these reasons, then shame on you. While we all need to earn a respectable living and want to take care of our families, and ourselves, we also need to look at the bigger picture.

The fire service is here to take care of others that cannot take care of themselves, and who call us when they are having one of the worst days of their lives. You have to want to help people and solve their problems in times of need (just don't say you want to help people in the oral interview, it sounds cliché and is a clone answer that will make you sound like the majority of other candidates). Knowing as much as you can about the fire service and what a firefighter does will not only make you a more prepared candidate, but also a better firefighter once you get hired. We work for the customers that pay their taxes to subsidize us, and we are at their mercy. If they don't feel they need as many fire stations or firefighters as they currently have, and don't want to pay any more taxes, they can easily complain to their city leaders and ask for cutbacks. We don't ever want that to happen.

If you truly want to become a firefighter, I truly encourage you to embrace the career, the fire service, and learn as much as you can about what we do, how we work, whom we work for, and why we do what we do. This will help you tremendously in many ways, more than you can imagine. I am the type of person that wants to know about as much as I can about something when I get involved with it. When I started testing to become a firefighter, I jumped headfirst into the fire service and tried to learn as much as I could about it, and have never stopped. I keep asking questions as to why things occur, why we do (or don't do) things a certain why, and the list goes on.

Some ways to learn more about the fire service include, but are not limited to:

- Visiting fire stations.
- Talking with firefighters.
- Visiting Fire Department websites.
- Visiting fire service related websites (magazines, associations, organizations, fire buff sites, etc.).
- Subscribing to fire service publications and email lists.
- Talking with other future firefighters while going through classes with them or while at fire department tests.

A critical failure made by many firefighter candidates is not taking the proper time to educate themselves on the fire service and the career they aspiring to. Don't expect the department hiring you to provide the information, even the basic information. Many departments expect you to know some basics, such as:

- The difference between an Engine and a Truck.
- The typical role of a firefighter.
- The typical daily routine of a firefighter.

- Thy typical services a fire department offers its citizens.
- Basic staffing levels.
- Basic fire department rank structure.
- Basic city department rank structure.

Part of your research is to see how fire departments tend to differ from each other in the following manners:

- Services provided.
- Staffing levels.
- Rank structure.
- Career opportunities.
- Terminology utilized.

Why is it important to know how departments differ? When you are participating in their testing process, you want to use the proper terminology to show that you have actually done some research!

Why Should I Obtain Formal Fire Related Education?

You may be thinking by now, why should I obtain formal fire related education when most fire departments typically don't require any college degree, let alone formal education to apply for the position of firefighter?

I hear these questions almost weekly:

1. "Do I really need to finish my two year degree?"
2. "Why do I need a degree to become a firefighter – it's just a blue color job?"
3. "I have my two year degree already, isn't that enough?"
4. "I have a four year degree from somewhere, isn't that enough?"
5. "I don't ever want to become a fire chief or promote in the fire service. Why do I need to complete a degree?"
6. "Can I get hired as a firefighter without a degree?"
7. "I don't have time to get a degree."
8. "I want to become a firefighter. Can I do it with just completing my EMT and firefighter 1 academy certificates?"
9. "I have completed my two-year degree in fire technology and want to get a four-year degree now. Should I also get it in fire technology?"

Let me try to address these frequently asked questions to help spread some light on the subject. Education is very near and dear to my heart, so realize these are only my opinions based on my experience.

Question #1: "Do I really need to finish my two-year degree?"

Yes, you do. Even though most departments do not require a two or four-year degree to take their examination, the most competitive and successful candidates will usually have one or the other. Plus, it is very possible you will learn more in your two-year fire technology degree program than most fire departments can ever teach you in their academy, and even after their academy and during the course of your career.

Question #2: "Why do I need a degree to become a firefighter – it's just a blue collar job?"

Technically most departments only require someone to be 18 or 21 years and possess a G.E.D. or high school diploma to get hired. Realize that is the MINIMUM. Do you really want to be someone that gets through life using "minimum criteria" or do you want to be one that raises the bar and has higher expectations? Even though that is the minimum, it is not uncommon to see departments advertise that they also have "desirable qualifications" that can include education in some form, including having completed a degree. Yes, we are in effect a blue color job, but because of the excellent pay, benefits, and working conditions (I know that can be debatable) we tend to have a lot of candidates to pick from. When you have a large number of candidates to typically pick from, and because of what we have to offer, we have the ability to pick the best of the best, and the ones that have a significant amount of education. Additionally, having a degree shows some commitment and motivation among other things.

Question #3: "I have my two-year degree already, isn't that enough?"

It all depends what your two-year degree is in. If it is a non-fire field, than by all means try to get one in fire to show your commitment and dedication to our industry. If it is in a fire related field, then congratulations for going this far. If you want to become a paramedic or become bilingual, then I would say hold off on the four-year degree and get one or both of those items completed. I would say more fire departments look for someone that is a paramedic or is bilingual before they look for someone who has a four-year degree (at least in California). However, if you don't want to become a paramedic or become bilingual (in any language), then you need to find a way to continue your education.

Question #4: "I have a four-year degree from somewhere, isn't that enough?"

In my opinion, no it is not enough. Why? Because that four-year degree is probably in a field other than fire and it doesn't show your commitment to the fire service. It shows your commitment to whatever that field you got the degree in. Don't get me wrong; a four-year degree in anything is better than a four-year degree in nothing. However, take the time to also get a two-year degree in fire to show your commitment to our line of work. The additional education will be very helpful to your future success.

Question #5: "I don't ever want to become a fire chief or promote in the fire service. Why do I need to complete a degree?"

Think back 10 or 20 or 25 years (if you are even that old). Do you think your thoughts, viewpoints, desires, career goals, etc. have changed? I bet they have. Just because you say one thing now, it doesn't mean your mind won't change later in life after you have been afforded more experience, more knowledge, etc. I have seen countless people in life that have said "I only wish I would have done this or done that." Don't let yourself get in that position. Properly prepare yourself for the future and provide yourself with tools to succeed (such as a degree). I have seen many people change their minds in life because of their current family situation or just for a change of heart.

Question #6: "Can I get hired as a firefighter without a degree?"

Yes, but your chances greatly increase by having at least a two-year degree in something. It is not the degree that gets you hired, it is doing exceptionally well on the oral interview which usually makes up 100% of your final score / ranking on the hiring list. However, if you do have education, it typically can only help you score higher in the oral.

NOTE: please don't think having a two or four-year degree will guarantee you a job or a high score on the oral. I've seen people that have awesome resumes never score in the top ranks because they can't sell themselves or properly market themselves.

Question #7: "I don't have time to get a degree."

Who does have enough time? Bottom line – make the time, quit making excuses and just do it. Time never seems to get more abundant as you get older and more involved in whatever your life contains. I was able to complete my two-year degree in fire technology while working full-time, volunteering my time at various events, and testing at every fire department I qualified for. I was able to complete my four-year degree while working full time at Longs Drugs Stores in a management position. Lastly, I was able to complete my master's degree while working full time as a fire captain, working full-time at the college as an instructor / fire technology coordinator, and still maintaining a healthy and happy marriage. I wanted it bad enough; I found the time and made it happen. It wasn't easy, but what is? If you want it bad enough, you'll find a way to make the time, bottom line.

Question #8: "I want to become a firefighter. Can I do it with just completing my EMT or firefighter 1 academy certificates?"

Nothing in life is impossible. However, your chances are not as good as if you have put more time and energy into your preparation for the career. If you want to get by with only those two certificates, then you better have excellent oral interview skills (which most people don't) and you better make yourself marketable and unique to the fire service in such a way that we will hire you with only those two certificates.

Question #9: I have completed my two-year degree in fire technology and want to get a four-year degree now. Should I also get it in fire technology?

Definitely get your four year degree if you can make it work into your schedule, but I would encourage you to get it in a discipline that is not specifically fire related, but something broader. Don't get me wrong; a four-year degree in something is better than a four-year degree in nothing. But, if you have the choice, think about it and do what you think is appropriate. Here are my thoughts on what discipline it should be in and why:

- Having a four-year degree in fire can be considered too narrow or focused, even if you want to promote.
- If you look at many chief officer job flyers across the country, they typically look for a four-year degree (or higher) in fire, public administration, business administration, or any closely related field. Ok, when they say "closely related field," to me that can almost mean anything, because any four-year degree can be related to the fire service if you do it properly. As a chief officer, especially the higher up you go, they are looking for a broader range of education to fall back on, not just specific to fire. They're looking for people with a great knowledge of leadership, management skills, budgeting, people skills, communication

skills, problem solving skills, and team-building skills, just to name a few.

- Get your four-year degree in something that you find interesting and can also be marketable if you ever get injured on the job and are retired out at an early age (yes that does happen) and have to find another job to pay the bills, or to use when you get retired. While a four-year degree in fire might be great for the fire department (don't get me wrong, it is still a good degree to have, but if you have the option....) trying to use it in the outside world to get a job is not going to provide you with many marketable skills. On the other hand, having a degree in business administration or some other similar field will leave you with many options.

Why Go Through A College Fire Academy?

If the fire department that hires me will put me through their own recruit academy (and pay me for it), why should I waste my time in advance going through a college fire academy?

Many future firefighters ask me why they should go through a college fire academy when the department that hires them will also put them through an academy. I guess they feel it is something redundant that is unnecessary or a waste of time. In reality, not going through a college fire academy prior to getting hired by a fire department will actually put you at a disadvantage when you do get hired.

Think of going through a college fire academy as the same as playing college baseball and / or minor league baseball prior to getting called up to the major leagues. How many sports stars do you know that went straight from high school to the pros? Very few I bet. Now of those that you do know, how many actually had successful, long-lasting careers in the pros? Even fewer I bet. Most of the successful professional sports stars have done their time playing not only college ball but also playing some form of minor league/amateur level ball as well.

In sports, playing ball at the college and/or minor league/amateur level can be considered a grooming or preparation time for the player. That time before they reach the professional level is meant to fine-tune them, work on their weaknesses, and capitalize on their strengths. Practice makes perfect, and that is what this quality time should be thought as. Think of going to a college fire academy in the same fashion. Nobody is perfect; because of that, we are all going to make mistakes and have things we are strong at and things we are weak at.

I am very happy that I went through a college fire academy prior to getting hired with the department I work for and prior to having to go also go through our academy. While I definitely did not know everything there was to be a firefighter, it was very comforting to be going through basically the same training that I had done a few years prior at the college fire academy. When I was hired, of the 11 of us hired, I believe only a few of us had actually gone through another fire academy prior to their getting hired. For those that had already gone through another fire academy, and were taking their second or third academy now, the experience was minimally stressful.

However, some of the recruits I was hired with had never been through a fire academy of any kind, and some of them had zero or minimal fire related education to provide and fall back on. While there were some exceptions, it was pretty obvious to pick out who had previously been through an academy and who had not, based on the performances demonstrated – both in the classroom and on the drill ground.

Think of it this way. You have finally obtained the dream job of your life – being a firefighter. Why would you want to risk getting terminated during the academy and/or probation for poor performance? Yes, there are many departments that have no problem releasing (terminating) recruits during the academy and/or during probation for poor performance issues (among other things). Most departments require you to keep an 80% average on your written tests during the academy and/or probation. Are you able to do that now? If you are unable to do that now, how do you think you are going to be able to do that once you get hired and are faced with a more stressful and challenging environment?

In my opinion, here are the advantages of going through a college fire academy prior to getting hired by a fire department:

1. Many departments require a candidate to have completed a

college fire academy and/or have their state firefighter 1 certificate just to apply to their department. Not having completed an academy may keep you from taking a number of tests.

2. Even if a department is going to put you through their own academy upon hiring, realize that having at least one college fire academy under your belt can only help you succeed in the one your dream department puts you through.

3. You have already seen and experienced a good majority of the curriculum you will be tested on. Remember that practice makes perfect and redundancy is beneficial to learning and retention. If you have done well on something the first time during the college fire academy, you should also do well during the department's academy.

4. You are in some ways, a proven commodity. Demonstrating that you have been through a college fire academy demonstrates to a fire department that you can do it and that you have what it takes. No department wants to hire people just to have to terminate them for poor performance. It is very costly to hire someone and then terminate them.

5. Many college fire academies are tougher than some paid fire department's recruit academies. I know this sounds strange, but it is true. I know of many college fire academies that have extremely tough standards, and do not tolerate poor performance (meaning they do not spoon-feed the students). Many fire departments and fire service personnel are also aware of the reputations that college fire academies have and may even give those students a preference when it comes to hiring.

Fire Technology Related Educational Opportunities

Many community colleges across the United States offer Fire Technology (or Fire Science, or some other closely related name) programs to complete your two-year degree. If you want to become a firefighter, I encourage you to immediately enroll in your local community college offering such a program. I was fortunate to have about seven different colleges within an hour drive of my residence, when I started to test, and even more fortunate to have a college within 15 minutes, where I ended up getting my two year degree, EMT certification, and firefighter 1 academy certification.

If you are wondering where to find community colleges offering fire technology education, consider:

- Talking to firefighters at your local fire department; many of them probably graduated from the local colleges and / or know of the local colleges offering such programs.
- Visit the websites of your local fire departments; many of them have firefighter recruitment information on there as well as contact information for the local programs.
- Visit the Perfect Firefighter Candidate website at http://www. firecareers.com – they have a listing of fire technology related educational institutions from virtually every state in the United States.

When you find a college to attend, take the following information into consideration:

- Most fire technology programs are very impacted, meaning they are overfilled (the demand exceeds the supply) and some have waiting lists to get in.
- Most colleges only start three times per year: summer, fall or spring. That means, depending on timing, you might be only able to start in June, August or January. About two weeks into every semester, I get many phone calls from students asking if it is too late to get into the current semester (yes, it is. We're already overbooked and it is hard to have someone start after missing the first two weeks). I tell them they have to wait until the next semester starts, which is typically four months away. I hear every sob story in the book as to how this will ruin their life, and so on. I try to explain this won't ruin their life, and that they can do many things to help prepare themselves for

the next semester, including visiting fire stations, researching and educating themselves on the fire service, volunteering their time, etc.

- Attempt to contact the fire technology coordinator (the person in charge of the program) and see if they have a website for the program that provides a good semester-by-semester plan of action for you to schedule your classes. See if you can make an appointment with them and find out more about the career and what the college has to offer. Most fire technology coordinators are either retired or active fire service professionals from the local departments, with great advice to offer.

- Realize that you may have to alter your work schedule to take some of the classes. Take a look at the previous semester's schedule to see what times/days the classes are offered and hopefully you have a great working relationship with your employer to allow some flexibility in scheduling. Remember that you don't want to burn your current employer; you need to stay on their good side as you will be using them for a reference in the future. Try to give them solutions, not problems. I used to try and give my employer my fire schedule for the next six months so they could plan around it. I also didn't expect them to do that for me, I asked and hoped they would do it for me (remember, we're not entitled to anything in life). Be up front with your current employer about your career aspirations and don't be surprised if they get mad or disappointed with you for wanting to leave them (can you blame them?).

- Have backup plans in place. Meaning, research multiple colleges so you don't rely on one college for everything. Be careful though, some classes may not transfer from college to college; it is pretty much up to each fire technology coordinator to allow classes to transfer in; additionally, in California, a student has to have at least 12 units in that major at that college to get a degree from a certain college.

- I have had students come to me wanting us to grant them a degree but when I go through their transcript, I see that they have completed about 9 units of fire classes at each college, but at no college have they done at least 12 units, and they have taken every fire class known to man. They can still file for a two-year degree in general studies, but not in the major they wanted (unless they take enough units at our college in fire, which they typically don't want to do at this point).

- Also, many colleges are "sister colleges," such as Chabot College in Hayward and Las Positas College in Livermore. We both offer the same fire classes, so a student can take classes at both colleges, depending on how the classes fit into their schedule and the availability of classes.

- Plus, what happens if you don't get into the classes you want, what are you going to do? Hopefully find other fire classes or general education classes to get out of the way. Instead, maybe spend the semester volunteering more hours or saving up money by working more hours so you can work fewer hours in the future. I can only speak for Chabot College, but our firefighter 1 academy and our EMT program fill up very quickly once registration opens up. Even the other fire related classes are usually full well before the first day of class. Just because a class is full doesn't mean you cannot add in if there are still seats available. But, not every instructor allows students to add in on the first day due to overcrowding issues and other reasons.

Successfully Passing Your Fire Technology Classes: Part 1

Many of you are either presently taking or planning to take fire technology classes at your local community college to prepare yourself to become a firefighter. I want to share some of my experience (19 plus years of teaching at the college level, 4 ½ of those years as a fire technology program coordinator and 7 years as an EMT program coordinator) so that you can learn from the mistakes of others and NOT follow in the same footsteps as those that have not succeeded.

One of the classes I am presently teaching is the Introduction to Fire Protection class. I get to see students in their first semester, many of them fresh out of high school and with no life experience to speak of (not that there is anything wrong with that). This can be rewarding, depending on the student. It is great seeing students succeed from their first class into a firefighter job a couple of years later - that is what makes my day.

We start with about 50 students on day one, and typically only graduate anywhere from 12 to 20 students, with the rest getting either an "F" or a "W" – for withdrawing or getting dropped before the end of the semester. These numbers are typical in our night class, but with a slightly higher success rate. I have been frustrated with the high failure rate, but based on this class being the first one in the fire series, it does make sense. Not everyone knows what they are getting into or if they actually want to be a firefighter. Obviously many students take one class (like the introduction class) and never take any other ones or even attempt to become a firefighter. That's ok, not everybody is cut out for every job.

One of my biggest frustrations is students that cannot follow simple directions or do not put their heart and soul into what they are trying to accomplish. We are not there to babysit or spoon-feed you, we are here to provide you with a rock-solid foundation to start off your fire service career and set you up for success. Do some of the instructors spoon-feed students? I would by fooling myself if I didn't say that it does occur not just at our college, but at most colleges nationwide. As instructors, we are not doing you the student any service spoon-feeding you.

Since my Introduction to Fire Protection Technology class starts with about 50 students, and there are probably only about 20 or so that really deserve to be there (deserve meaning they will do the best they can, they demonstrate potential, they take it serious, and in my eyes, they have a good shot at getting hired if they don't give up or do something stupid). I wish I could go right to that 20 or so that should be there and focus all of my efforts on seeing them succeed. Well, one of the things I require of students is that they pass the midterm with a grade of at least 80% (which is the very bottom of the "C" grade scale - 79% is a "D" grade, and a "D" or an "F" requires the student to take the class again if they want to proceed to the Firefighter 1 Academy). If they don't pass the midterm with at least 80%, they are advised that they can no longer stay in the class. The primary reason they are asked to leave is because if they're struggling to get at least 80% on the midterm, they'll more thank likely fail the final exam which is much tougher.

Well, let's take a step back. To even be eligible to take the midterm, a student must be passing all quizzes up to the midterm with at least a 70% score. Like above, the primary reason is that if they are struggling to get 70% on the quizzes up to the midterm, odds are they won't even be able to pass the midterm with an 80%, let alone make it all the way to the final and be fortunate enough to pass that with at least an 80%. As much as I would like to let a student go all the way through a class for the exposure, even they're tanking it, I think it's worse for someone to get dropped from class towards the end or get an "F" at the end. It's more heartbreaking than releasing them in the first half of the class. I've taught semester classes like this for over 15 years, and have seen thousands of students, so I have had a chance to see what works and what doesn't work, not to mention get a good idea on who will probably be successful in the end.

Well, there are some very common themes with virtually ALL of the students that failed the midterm and got dropped from the class that you can learn from. Most (if not all) of them would have been successful if they had:

1. Shown up at ALL class sessions. All of them had missed at least one day.
2. Shown up ON TIME to all class sessions. Most of them had been tardy to at least one session. The fire service does not appreciate tardiness.
3. Turned in ALL of their homework assignments. Here is one of the spoon-feeding things I have mixed feelings on: every week they get some questions to answer and turn in the next week. These questions are virtually the same as they see on the test next week. You would think that if you do the homework you would get 100% on the test, well, that is not the case. Homework is not required, but they get up to 5 extra credit points for doing the questions. Extra credit is only added in at the END of class after they have passed with at least a "C". ALL of the students who had failed the midterm had failed to turn in all or some of the homework assignments.
4. Passed the midterm. One of the reasons I would rather drop them if they fail the midterm is because if they fail the midterm, there is a very high chance they won't even get higher than a D in the class at the end. In the past, most of the students who failed the midterm (before we dropped them for this) failed the final and ended up with an F or a D. Only in rare circumstances did students get their act together and kick it into overdrive and pass with a C or better.
5. Passed the weekly quizzes with at least 80%. All of the students

we dropped had failed at least one quiz. Most of them had failed over half of the tests they had taken.

6. Turned in other assignments early or at least on time. Another interesting coincidence is that these same students were the same ones that turned in any special assignments (reports, etc.) late or at least attempted to turn them in late (we typically don't accept late stuff).

7. Taken responsibility for their actions (or lack of actions) and actually held themselves accountable. I've heard every excuse in the book and I bet I'll hear new ones every semester. Do you think the fire department that wants (or wanted) to hire you cares that you forgot to completely fill out the application or that your application was late because you forgot the final filing date?

I hand out a "Student Contract" on the first day of class to "lay the foundation and the ground rules" up front. They get a copy and they sign a copy for me to keep.

Below is an example of a student contract I previously used when I taught the morning session of the Introduction to Fire Protection class, and when we used to take quizzes in class and submit homework in class (quizzes are now done online prior to the start of class each week, as are the homework assignments).

Well, what are some of the items I put in the contract that will fail them? Here are the items:

Fire Technology 50 Student Contract

Following instructions (either oral or written) is paramount to your success as a future firefighter. Not properly following instructions on the fireground can lead to the death or serious injury of a fellow firefighter and/or yourself. Learning to follow instructions in this class will help you be a successful firefighter; an asset to yourself, your crew, and the citizens you provide service to.

I agree to abide by all of the requirements set forth in the course syllabus that was handed out on the first day of class, including (but not limited to) the following items:

- The GREEN 100 Question Scantron score sheets (Form 882-E) will be required for weekly quizzes, the Midterm examination, and the Final Examination. Turning in a Scantron that is not the required Scantron will result in my forfeiting points from that test for not following directions. Also, using anything but a #2 pencil to answer your questions that does not allow the Scantron machine to properly score your test will also result in your forfeiting the points from that test.

- All assignments, homework, projects, etc. are due at 8:00 a.m. at the start of class. Showing up late to class and turning in an assignment after 8:00 a.m. may result in your not receiving full credit for that assignment. If you show up on time you are assumed to have your required assignments with you at that time. No points will be given for homework, assignments, projects, etc. not turned in after the class for the day ends.

- I will show up to class by 8:00 a.m. so that I am not a disruption to the rest of the class or the instructor. Tests are usually administered right at 8:00 a.m.; If I arrive during the middle of a test, I may not be able to take the test or if I am allowed to take the test (at the instructor's discretion), I will only be allowed the remaining minutes allotted to the class that is presently taking the test. As soon as you walk into the class, please turn in any required homework or assignments onto the instructor's desk in the front of the room.

- All homework assignments and paperwork MUST be stapled if more than one page. Items not stapled will NOT be accepted.

- I understand that NO make-up quizzes will be given. If I arrive late to class and the quiz / examination has already been administered, I will not be able to receive the points for missing the quiz / examination.

- The trade article is due no later than the fifth class session. The trade article must be from a fire service related trade / technical publication, not from a general circulation newspaper such as the San Francisco Chronicle. Failure to turn in a trade article will result in your having to withdraw from the class with a "W."

- The rough draft of the group project MUST be turned in by the date requested. Failure to turn in the rough draft will result in your having to withdraw from the class with a "W."

- I may be dropped from the class if I miss 2 classes in a row, or 12 total hours. Time lost due to excessive tardiness or leaving the class early (unexcused) may count toward the 12 total hours.

- I will be dropped from the class if I do not show up at the first class meeting. This is necessary to make room for the students that do show up and want to add in. It is not fair to those folks wanting to add in to have to wait a week to see if there will be an open spot or not.

- I will be dropped from the class if I show up at the first class session, but then miss the second, class session.

- If I am given an add number by the instructor, I have no more than 24 hours from the end of the first class session to enroll in this class. Since class ends at noon on Monday, you have until noon on Tuesday, the next day, to utilize your add number. If you have problems using the add number, you need to contact the instructor a.s.a.p. Failing to contact the instructor by noon on Tuesday will result in your not being able to use the add number and not being able to continue in the class.

- I may be dropped from the class if I do not show up to take the midterm examination or if I do not receive a passing score on the midterm.

- I will turn off my cellular phone and / or pager when I am in the Fire Technology 50 class, so as to not disrupt the class. I understand that I will be given a verbal warning for failing to do so on the first occasion, and that on the second occasion; I will receive a written warning that will go in my class file. On the third occasion, I face being dropped from the class for failure to follow directions.

- I agree to be mature and take responsibility for my actions and not make excuses for why I did not complete something or why I failed to follow instructions.

- I understand that I must abide by the College rules regarding plagiarism and cheating. If I am caught cheating or plagiarizing anything, I will no longer be allowed to continue in the class. CHEATING AND/OR PLAGIARISM WILL NOT BE TOLERATED!

Some say it sounds too harsh or too strict. Well, if we as instructors do not properly lay the foundation for these future firefighters, they may not be fully prepared for the para-military environment they want to get into. I would rather have someone struggle and have a setback by failing a class NOW at the college level than after they get hired and are in the academy and/or probation. Failing something at that level may lead to termination. Failing things now still gives you time to regroup and get yourself back on course for success.

Some of these items in my contract might be petty. However, I want to get the students to actually read the fine print and most of all - LEARN TO FOLLOW DIRECTIONS! Many of us do not read instructions or directions. I bet every fire department has at least one firefighter that continuously demonstrates the inability to follow instructions, causing extra work for their supervisor or other individuals within the department. Some fire department recruit academies do a good job of weeding out those that can't. This way, by giving the student a contract on the first day, they see what will fail them and what will keep them in the class. There are no secrets. You either follow directions or you do not.

Just a lot of thoughts I wanted to pass on to help set you up for success. Learn from the mistakes of others and properly prepare yourself for a career as a firefighter! Now is the time to start off on the right foot!

Successfully Passing Your Fire Technology Classes: Part 2

About a month or two prior to the start of a new semester at the college, I obtain the email addresses of the students who have enrolled in my class and I take the time to send them a welcome email to allow them to start getting their head around what they're getting themselves into. I think this is especially critical because many of these students are entering college straight from high school and think that the fire technology classes are easy and not that difficult to do well at. Not sure where they get that idea?

It's actually interesting to watch the numbers of students registered in class actually drop after I email the below information to them. Why is that? Are they scared away at the upcoming workload? Are they being smart and realizing they're in over their head? Don't know. I do know I get a fair amount of email replies from students who actually thank me for sending this to them in advance so they can start preparing for class and what they are getting into.

Greetings Fire Technology 50 students!

First of all, let me introduce myself, I am your instructor for the Fire 50 class you have signed up for this upcoming semester starting at 1800 hours (6 pm) -**sharp**. Welcome to our program and to the Fire 50 class! Please plan to be at EVERY Monday session for Fire Technology 50.

Missing just one class can cause you to do poorly (including fail the class) and it is important that you sit and participate in EVERY class session to help prepare you to become a firefighter.

Please be familiar with the online program Blackboard (available on the college website) - as we will use that for all grading as well as some occasional assignments, such as group discussions or quizzes. It's pretty user friendly once you get used to it, so the sooner you start learning about how things work, the better off you'll be.

I have included your email address (which I obtained from college records only I have access to as your instructor and PROMISE not to share with anyone) in my free email mailing list that I use to send out fire job announcements, fire news stories, volunteer opportunities, etc. For more information on the email list and what I provide, visit your website for our program at http://www.chabotfire.com and scroll down and you'll see what this entails. **If for some reason you DO NOT want your name included on this email list, please let me know and I will remove your name.**

Your program website, http://www.chabotfire.com has numerous great resources for you, the future firefighter to start using. Some of the areas on the above website I encourage you to visit include:

1. **Chabot College Fire & EMS news** - a free monthly newsletter geared at better preparing you for a career in the fire service. I recently emailed you the latest issue and posted it on the website - (you'll receive future issues via email until you tell me to remove your name) please take a look at it - I think you'll find some worthwhile information inside. If you go to http://www.chabotfire.com you can view the current and older issues with valuable firefighter preparation information.

2. **"So, you want to become a firefighter? 5 guidelines to assist you in becoming a firefighter"** - this downloadable document has great tips you can follow to better prepare yourself for success in the process of becoming a firefighter, including what classes you should be taking.

3. **Firefighter Hiring Process Components** - a section dedicated

to the various components of the hiring process that you must successfully pass to get hired as a firefighter, such as the oral interview, written test, and background investigation. Many great links to helpful sites and many free articles of information to share with you.

4. **Website links** - an extensive links page of everything from fire departments to other colleges offering EMT, paramedic, and firefighter degree and academy programs. A great way to start educating yourself on the fire service.

5. **Firefighter 1 Certification and Academy information** - a section meant to educate you on the process of getting your firefighter 1 academy and firefighter 1 certification.

6. **EMT and Paramedic information** - a section dedicated to educate you on the process of becoming an EMT and/or paramedic.

7. **Fire related email lists** - many free email mailing lists (besides this one) to sign up for staying up-to-date with the fire service.

8. **Volunteer Opportunities** - links to various volunteer opportunities.

Regarding the Fire 50 class, for some, this may be one of the toughest classes you'll ever take; for some, it will be the easiest. It's up to you to be successful. We are not going to spoon-feed you or let you "just barely pass."

I will attach the student contract that we hand out on the first day so you can start to get a feel of what you're getting into. I encourage you to read it and email me if you have any questions.

This is not meant to scare you or turn you off as much as it is meant to motivate you to be the best you can be and ensure you have your act together: this class usually starts with about 50 students and only about 15 usually pass with a "C" or higher (you need a C or higher to go to the academy) - last semester, only about 10 passed with a C or higher. The rest got D's or F's. Why?

- Many people are fresh out of high school and not prepared for what they are getting into.
- Many people think that this will be easy and not require any work. Think again.

This class is not tough, and it is very easy and reasonable to pass with at least a C if you do the following things:

1. Show up to class every day, on time and stay for the entire length (6 pm to 10 pm).
2. Take every test and turn in every assignment on time or early.
3. Do the homework EVERY week.
4. Have a positive, can-do attitude.
5. Be a team player that is willing to form study groups with other students and work well with other students.
6. Pay attention in class.
7. Come to class prepared to learn.
8. Act mature and professional.
9. Do your assigned reading in advance of class (so you can ask questions and better understand the material).
10. Last but not least, start learning as much as you can about the fire service, by living, sleeping, eating and breathing becoming a firefighter.

Realize doing all of the above won't necessarily guarantee 100% success (because you still have to pass everything), but it will definitely increase your odds tremendously. Virtually everyone of the people that got an F or D violated many if not all of the 10 above items. I want to see ALL of you succeed, which is why I'm trying to prepare you up front of what you're getting into. The reason I'm sounding a little tough is because I may have to work with you one day at my department (and I want to make sure you have your act together), because you may get hired at some other department (and I want to keep our excellent reputation as a program), and because the public deserves the best service possible. I sure don't want someone coming to my house when

I call 9-1-1 that only passes with a 70% score. I want those that pass in the high 90's and have their act together. Don't you????

Also, our Firefighter 1 Academy (Fire 90A, 90B, 90C) typically starts with 35 students and graduates about 15 to 25 students. What are the biggest problems causing people to fail?

1. They cannot keep up the 80% average that is required on all weekly quizzes.
2. They cannot perform the physical ability portions of the academy.
3. They cannot do the skills required to do the job under stress.

That is why we are so tough on you in the beginning classes before the academy, to help not only prepare you for the job, but to prepare you for the academy and the EMT program (which has similar numbers). Some who have not been successful have said we are mean, and nothing could be farther from the truth; trust me. All of our instructors care about you and want you to succeed (assuming you are capable). I am rarely at school (outside of class) because of my fire department schedule, so the best way to contact me is to email me (or try me on my cell phone - but try email first - it comes to my cell phone and I can answer it pretty quickly); feel free to contact me if you have any questions or concerns. I look forward to meeting every one of you and will do my best to make you the best firefighter candidate you can be.

Lastly, we encourage you to purchase the books for the class. To find out what books are needed, you can visit the Chabot College bookstore online or go in person and find what is necessary. Please double check the college website for more info so you don't waste a trip. Since there is a quiz the second Monday (and every Monday after that), it's critical to get the books PRIOR to the start of class so you can get a head start on the huge amount of reading that is necessary.

Here are the required textbooks:

1. IFSTA, Orientation and Terminology, Fifth Edition.
2. CFFJAC, Diversity: The Impact of Perceptions, 1995.

Item 1 above can be purchased at normal book outlets.

Item 2 above can only be purchased through the Chabot bookstore.

Before you think this is going to be "too tough" - well think of this...
if it were easy to become a firefighter, then everybody would be getting
hired - which we know is not the case. Nothing worth having in life
comes easy, and good things come to those who wait. Don't expect the
career to come easily or quickly; if it does, it's probably too good to be
true and over the long haul, you won't be as successful as the person
who obtained the career the slow, methodical and persistent way, not
rushing but not sitting back waiting for it to happen without doing
anything to make it happen.

However, I can only do so much - **it's up to you to actually do the
work and not give up!** Thanks for listening, see you in class - I look
forward to meeting and working with each of you!

Take care,
Steve

EMS Related Training For
Future Firefighters

Virtually every fire department across the United States responds to Emergency Medical Service (EMS) calls, and in most departments, EMS calls make up 70 to 80% of their call volume. Because of this, many fire departments only hire people with EMS certifications, to help reduce their training costs and narrow down the pool of candidates to a more manageable level. The three most common certifications/licenses required by fire departments include:

- Cardio Pulmonary Resuscitation (CPR)
- Emergency Medical Technician (EMT)
- Paramedic

CPR Certification:

CPR certification is usually the first steps of medical related training for a firefighter. CPR training may be found at a number of different locations, such as a community college, at your local community center (found through your city government), your local fire department, or through a private company. Nationwide associations or organizations such as the American Red Cross and the American Heart Association also offer such training. CPR training may be a part of a Standard or Advanced First Aid Training class, or a stand-alone class. CPR certification is usually good for one or two years, depending on where it is taken. There also may be various levels of CPR certification, so ensure you do your homework before signing up for a class.

EMT-Basic Certification:

EMT-Basic training is typically at least 110 hours in length, and includes a combination of classroom lecture, skills demonstrations and evaluations, and patient contact time on a fire engine or ambulance. EMT training can be found at most colleges that offer fire technology education, as well as private institutions. EMT certificates are typically valid for two years and are not necessarily transferable from state-to-state.

Prerequisites to get into EMT programs can vary. At Chabot College, we require the following of a person wanting to get into the EMT program:

1. Current CPR certification. Must be either CPR for the Professional Rescuer by the American Red Cross OR BLS – Healthcare Provider by the American Heart Association.
2. Completion of the Emergency Response course (also known as "EMS First Responder"), a minimum 53 hour class that includes the above CPR certification as well as introduces the student to the majority of the skills and topics found in the EMT program. Basically a mini EMT class.
3. Proof of the following immunizations:
   - Tuberculosis (TB) test – no older than 12 months.
   - Measles, Mumps and Rubella.
   - Hepatitis B vaccination.

If you are thinking about taking your EMT training in one state, but eventually moving to another state, find out the requirements of that state you plan to move to by checking their State EMS Agency's website. Every state is different, and has different requirements as to what certificates are transferable. Also, consider taking a National Registry EMT certification exam (written test and skills evaluation) that is offered at various locations since most states accept a National Registry EMT certificate when someone wants to transfer in and work in their state.

Paramedic Licensure:

Paramedic programs consist of three components: didactic training (classroom), hospital clinical time, and field internship time. Paramedic programs typically last 6 to 18 months, can be part-time or full-time, and can include well over 1,000 hours of overall training. Paramedic programs are not easy, and it is paramount that you are well prepared for what you are getting yourself into. Personally, I felt paramedic school was tougher than four years of college when I was studying for my Bachelor of Science degree.

Prerequisites to get into paramedic programs can also vary; some programs require students to have EMT experience, such as working on an ambulance in a 9-1-1 system (responding with lights and siren, supporting fire department first responders, and then transporting patients to the most appropriate hospital) for at least 6 months. Even if you find a paramedic program that will let you in without the EMT experience, I would highly discourage you from attending until you have some good, solid EMT experience. How do you expect to be a good (not great) paramedic, if you were never a great EMT? Remember, if you are not using your skills, you will lose them and the knowledge learned within your EMT class within 30 days.

Would you like a paramedic working on you or a loved one that went straight from EMT training to paramedic training, and never had a chance to hone their skills working as an EMT? I wouldn't. There's a saying we have in the EMS world: paramedics save lives and EMTs save paramedics. What that means is that Basic Life Support (BLS), what an EMT does, is the cornerstone of EMS. Yes, Advanced Life Support (ALS) provided by paramedics may save lives, but without good, solid EMTs, nobody wins.

You Want To Become A Firefighter –
Should You Become A Paramedic?

Becoming a firefighter is not an easy task. Thousands of people lined up to take a test for a fire department that was only going to have a couple of job openings over the life of the list (if even that sometimes). I remember it so clearly. 3,000 people for one job; 5,000 people for 10 jobs; 4,000 people just so a fire department can establish a hiring list (but with no anticipation of hiring anyone). The list goes on and on. It was very intimidating at first seeing all of those people lined up and realizing I had to compete against all of them. It took me a while to figure it out, but I eventually did: I wasn't competing against them; I was competing against myself! I had nobody to blame except for myself if I did not get hired.

It did not take long to realize that those departments that were requiring candidates to be licensed as a paramedic (which more and more departments were starting to do in the early 1990's), even in the Bay Area, were getting less than 100 applicants every time they tested! Some departments were getting less than 50 applicants, and some as few as 10 to 20 applicants! If I really wanted to increase my odds of getting hired as a firefighter, I needed to become a paramedic.

When I began the process of becoming a firefighter, most of the firefighters I talked to all advised me to just go to the community college that has the fire technology program, and then get your EMT and your Firefighter 1 academy certificates and that should be all you need to get hired. Well, I soon found out what had worked for them when they got hired, was probably not going to work for me. Instead, I was going to do that and more! When my buddy Greg Vitz and I graduated with our four-year degrees from the local State University, we knew we wanted to become firefighters and started to draw out our plan of action after having conversations with various firefighters.

We knew that we would have to get our EMT certificate and Firefighter 1 certificate as soon as possible, so that we would be able to take more entry-level firefighter examinations (since that is what many of the Bay Area agencies were requiring to test). We knew we would also need to get our two-year degrees in Fire Technology as well, to help show our commitment to the fire service as well as our motivation. Our four year degrees were something we were proud of, but we also knew that some candidates did not have that level of education and we did not want to stand out too much and be considered as "over-educated" college boys that wanted to go straight to fire chief after probation.

That is why we knew we also had to get our two-year degrees in Fire Technology. We also knew that if we didn't get hired after receiving our EMT and Firefighter 1 academy certificates that we better bite the bullet and go to paramedic school. Obviously we were taking every test we qualified for and hoping we could get hired without becoming a paramedic. Not that we didn't want to become paramedics, we didn't want to endure another year or more of intense schooling. Don't get me wrong, it's not that we mind running EMS calls, however given the choice, I think we both would rather fight fire than run EMS calls (and that is probably true for many candidates that end up going to paramedic school).

This is where the problem begins for many future paramedic students. Many of them (like myself) go into paramedic school thinking it will be a quick and easy ticket into the fire service. Yes and no. Yes, your odds will greatly increase at getting into the fire service because you are a paramedic. No, because many students that go into paramedic school know that it is an easy ticket and do it just to become firefighters. I was one of those people. I went to paramedic school to become a firefighter. I will admit it.

However I soon realized that I wasn't going to get spoon fed the information and that I was going to have to work at becoming a paramedic. When it was all said and done, I still feel that paramedic school was tougher than going through and completing my four-year degree at California State University at Hayward! It was especially tough because I did not have a lot of experience working as an EMT to fall back on. I had no past experience working on an ambulance and I think it really hurt me and made me work harder than I probably should have. It makes sense now, when I look back at the situation: how did I expect to be a good paramedic, if I had never learned to become an excellent EMT? We're taught to crawl, and then walk. It was like an amateur athlete competing in a triathlon without ever becoming an excellent swimmer, bicyclist, and/or runner! Think of paramedic school the same way. Did I complete it? Yes; but it wasn't easy.

When I started paramedic school, it dawned on my very quickly that I had to become a paramedic because I wanted to become a paramedic, not because I wanted to become a firefighter. I had to acknowledge that while my ultimate long-term goal was to become a firefighter, for my short and medium range goals, I needed to work at being the best paramedic I could be. After talking to many paramedics and nurses that work in the field as preceptors in both hospitals and on ambulances, I started to realize that there was a significant failure rate when going through paramedic school, and that many of the students failed during the field internship phase.

Further investigation led me to understand why students were failing. Many of them had never worked as an EMT, and/or on an ambulance! Besides not having the prior experience, paramedic students were also at a disadvantage because many of the preceptors were sick and tired of students becoming paramedics just to become firefighters. They wanted people to be like they were when they were going to paramedic school, which was working at becoming the best paramedic they could be when they ultimately worked for the private ambulance company (because that is where most of the paramedic jobs were). In some ways, I can't blame the preceptors for not wanting to take students without

EMT experience, or being even harder on them for not having EMT experience.

I had started out in paramedic school like many students probably do. I had thought I could "skate" through the class work, get the license, get on a fire department, and do what I had to do to get by until the ambulance arrived or I didn't have to be a paramedic anymore. Reality soon set in after talking to many working firefighter / paramedics and private ambulance paramedics that advised me that I better become a paramedic because I want to, not because I have to. There was too much at risk if I didn't have my heart into it. It did not take much to lose your paramedic license (versus your EMT certificate); giving the wrong medication, not giving any medication, giving too much medication, not placing the Endotracheal tube in the right place, and the list goes on and on. All of those things could lead to losing my license.

Well, I'm not a genius, but I did see that if I did not complete paramedic school, or if I lost my paramedic license because of one of those above-mentioned items, I would probably never, ever, get another job as a paramedic or firefighter. I didn't like that thought. There is too much liability and at stake for a paramedic to be doing what they do if their heart and soul is not into it.

Also, I started seeing that many fire departments required their paramedics to be paramedics for a set number of years: 3 years, 5 years, 10 years, their entire career, until they promote, etc. I had to take a long look at the situation. Could I be a paramedic and be miserable for the next 30 years (because I did it just to become a firefighter) or could I embrace it and make the best of it? I chose to make the best of it and embrace it and attempt to be the best darn paramedic I could be, and I am glad I did so. If I truly wanted to be a firefighter, but I had to be a paramedic for my entire career, would that have worked for me? Yes, because my ultimate goal was to be a firefighter. Not everyone is willing to make that commitment though, and that is something you need to evaluate.

One preceptor told me, "When you start your field internship, you should be able to hit the ground running as a safe EMT, and a beginning paramedic. I first test you on your basic EMT skills to confirm your competency, and then let you start adding your paramedic skills. The last thing I want to be doing on your first few shifts is to be teaching you how to use a gurney or how to use your EMT skills that you had never used before (outside of the classroom). That takes up valuable training time that we don't have to spare." I couldn't agree with him more. Because of the glut of EMT students without experience, I could see how many of the preceptors were getting frustrated, not wanting to take students without experience, not wanting to pass them because they weren't even competent EMT's, and how students were failing their internships.

I didn't want to be one of those students! I had too much invested in becoming a firefighter to let this happen. I think I could have eventually been hired as a firefighter had I not completed paramedic school. However, I do know it would have taken me a lot longer than it actually did.

Here is how becoming a paramedic (and attempting to be the best paramedic I could be) worked for me. I took the test for the department I presently work for twice (once every two years). Both times, there were about 3,000 people testing for about 10 or so jobs. Both times, the department held a random lottery to reduce the numbers. Both times I was not selected in that random lottery. Both times, the department hired a fair amount of volunteers. Then, a miracle (for me) happened. The department was planning on providing paramedic services and needed to hire 11 paramedics. I got a letter in the mail one day stating that information, but I figured I didn't have a chance because I wasn't a volunteer there and because they were probably still going to have a lottery. Boy was I wrong. I found out there were less than 100 applicants that had even kept their contact information current and bothered to send copies of their paramedic licenses in.

They invited us to go to a physical ability test (because all original 3,000 or so had taken the written examination a year or so prior), and then if we were successful in that phase, to an oral interview. I still wasn't getting my hopes up. That was until I showed up at the physical ability test and found out there were about 70 candidates that had showed up. I further found out a few days later that only 60 went to the oral interviews; 60 people for 11 spots! Got to love those odds! I especially loved those odds since I was one of those lucky 11 individuals to go to the recruit academy.

One of the significant reasons I was able to get hired by my department was because I had made the effort and sacrifices to go through paramedic school. Yes, it cost me about $7,000 in tuition and books, as well as an undetermined cost of lost wages (because I could not work that many hours - I wanted to focus on paramedic school), but I easily made that up in my first year or so on the department. Money well spent, I might add.

Even now, becoming a paramedic is almost a sure way (I say almost because nothing in life is guaranteed and you can't count your chickens until they're hatched) onto the fire department. If you are willing to make a sacrifice for a year or so, spend the money necessary to get you from start to finish, dedicate yourself to becoming the best paramedic you can be, understand that you might have to be a paramedic for the duration of your employment with a fire department, then you significantly increase your odds of becoming a full-time firefighter. You make the choice; there is no one to blame but yourself if you never achieve each and every one of your dreams over the course of your lifetime!

I am not trying to tell you what to do. Your choice of becoming a paramedic or not becoming a paramedic is one only you can make. Either way, you have to live with your decision for the rest of your life. Do what you have to do to get what you want out of life. Just remember that if you do decide to do something and your heart and soul is not 100% into it, you are setting yourself (and your employer, and the public, and your co-workers) up for FAILURE! You need to do your best and set yourself up for success - the people we provide service to deserve nothing less than the best!

How To Properly Present Yourself During A Fire Station Visit

Visiting a fire station can be a very educational and rewarding experience when you are testing to become a firefighter. However, if you are not careful, the impression you make, as well as the behavior you present, may actually go against you when it comes to getting a job with that fire department. I am a firm believer that you don't get a second chance to make a first impression. Why would you even want to visit a fire station you might wonder?

Here are the three main reasons why you would visit a fire station:

1. To find out more about the job and the career of a firefighter.
2. To obtain more information about that fire department preferably before they offer a firefighter examination (I say before because once a fire department opens up their firefighter examination process, everybody and their brother and sister will come out of the woodwork to start visiting fire stations, and because some departments don't allow station visits during the examination process).
3. To start building and maintaining positive working relationships with those in the fire service (networking).

What benefits can you receive out of visiting a fire station?

- Getting the chance to network, make friends, and make contacts that may be able to assist you in the future. Even if that fire department doesn't hold a firefighter exam for the next few years, I bet many of those firefighters have friends or relatives that work on many other neighboring fire departments that they can put you in touch with for assistance.
- Getting the chance to learn more about the job and the career of a firefighter.
- Getting the chance to ask questions of the firefighters that you may have not been able to find answers for on the department website or through other methods.
- Getting the chance to meet firefighters that may be sitting on your oral interview panel either in that department or a neighboring department (I've lost count of the amount of times I visited fire stations when I was testing for firefighter positions and I ran into someone who was going to be on the oral board – even though I did not know it at the time of the station visit).
- Getting the chance to talk to the newly hired firefighters so that you can ask them questions relating to what they did to get hired, and to find out what information they can share with you that might assist you in your pursuit.

What types of questions should I <u>NOT</u> ask the firefighters?

- How many stations does your department have?
- How many personnel are on the department?
- How many square miles does the department protect?
- What is the population the department protects?
- What is the name of the Fire Chief?
- Do you know how many people you are planning on hiring?
- What is the salary of a firefighter?
- How many vacation days do firefighters get?
- What other benefits does a firefighter receive?

Now you may wonder why I say don't ask those questions since they appear to be questions worth asking or questions I'll need to have the answer for, right? Well, yes and no. Most of those questions can be answered by doing some basic research on the Internet. The questions regarding the department can usually be found on the fire department website (official or unofficial). The questions regarding salary and benefits are those taboo questions that really don't matter. If you want to be a firefighter bad enough, you're not going to care about the salary and/or the benefits. Right? Or are you just in this for the time off, the money and/or the benefits? Well?

Don't get me wrong; you'll need to obtain the answers to those above questions for every department you apply for. However, a lot of that information can be obtained from the fire department website, the city website, the actual job announcement and the human resources/personnel department website.

What types of questions should I ask the firefighters?

This is where many candidates drop the ball and waste the time of the firefighters they encounter. Instead of asking those questions you can probably find the answer for on the Internet or through other forms of basic research (like those mentioned above), I would encourage you to ask questions such as these:

- How does your department differ from other neighboring departments?
- Would it be possible to get a tour of the fire station and the apparatus?
- What do you like about working for this department/city?
- What do you dislike about working for this department/city?
- What do you think your department does well?
- What do you think your department could improve upon?
- Do you have any advice for me as an aspiring firefighter?
- Here is my resume; do you have any suggestions for me to improve my chances of becoming a firefighter?
- What does your department typically look for in firefighters?

- Are there any other stations, crews and/or personnel I should visit that you feel would benefit me in my preparation to become a firefighter?

Here are some suggestions to ensure that you make a good impression and that you properly present yourself to the firefighters:

Try not to just "drop in" and say, "can I get some of your time?"

Many crews have very busy schedules during the day and like to plan out their daily routine as best as they can. Some departments require that you contact the fire department administration office to make an appointment to visit a fire station. If you're not sure, just stop by a fire station and ask them if you could make an appointment for a station tour and a chance to ask them some questions about becoming a firefighter. They will either schedule an appointment, or if they have the time, fit you in right there.

If at all possible, attempt to call the station in advance to set up an appointment.

Some departments provide station phone numbers to the public; some do not provide station phone numbers to the public. It wouldn't hurt to stop by administration (headquarters) or a fire station and ask them for an address and phone list of all of their fire stations if you cannot locate such on the Internet. Let them know you want to become a firefighter and that you want to learn more about the job, and that you want to have a chance to talk to the firefighters. Because of heightened security measures these days, don't be surprised if they don't give out phone numbers. The worse thing they could say is no.

If they don't give you the station addresses, where can you find them?

Many fire departments list their fire station addresses on their website. Worse comes to worse, the Internet should be able to assist you if you search in the right places.

Whenever you stop by a fire station, bring a nice dessert. If you bring ice cream, don't bring the square stuff.

I laughed when I heard Captain Bob Smith mentioning on one of his audiotapes to not bring the square boxes of ice cream - bring the round containers. How true that is. I realize it is the thought that counts, but it just comes across as tacky or cheap (in my opinion), if you bring the cheap stuff. If you have the chance, bake something nice (like a cake, pie, or chocolate chip cookies - you can never go wrong with chocolate chip cookies!). Doing so shows a little more personalization and also demonstrates your cooking ability (or lack of ability). Make sure you bring enough for everyone that day on duty. Most fire stations only have three or four members on duty per day. One container of ice cream or one pie should suffice. However, if there are 10 or more firefighters on duty, don't walk in with one container of ice cream. Do your homework in advance; if worse comes to worse, count the cars in the fire station parking lot - which might give you a good clue. Now the square (or rectangular) boxes are OK if they're high quality ice cream such as Dreyers or Breyers, as opposed to the generic brands.

If you set up an appointment - DO NOT BE LATE!

This is a double standard. The firefighters can be late because that is their job! I remember a candidate showing up at 1:00 p.m. like I had asked him to. He had to wait out front until 2:00 p.m. because we were on a grass fire response. When we came back, he appeared to be perturbed that we were not there at 1:00 p.m. I kindly explained we HAD WORK TO DO, but he still seemed to be bitter and bent out of shape. Luckily he didn't get hired, because with an attitude like that, I bet he would have been a joy to be around at the station. He would have been the gift that kept on giving. If the firefighters aren't there when you are, then kindly wait. Give them time to return, and if you find yourself having to leave, at least leave a nice note on the door saying that you waited but you had another appointment (or something important) you had to leave for and that you would like to arrange another meeting some time in the future. Leave them your phone number. That shows respect and common courtesy.

When you are at the station, make the attempt to say hi, introduce yourself, and shake the hand of everyone present that day.

You never know where you might see that person again. By showing your politeness and enthusiasm at meeting the different firefighters, you show a positive and can-do attitude, not to mention you show that you are personable and approachable.

When you arrive, already have a list of questions that you want to have answered.

Also, bring a notebook and multiple pens (multiple because I have had numerous ones run out of ink and it is embarrassing to have to ask to borrow a pen). I mention the notebook as well because I had a candidate stop by and 30 minutes into the question and answer session he asked me if he could have a pen and paper to right down all of this good information I was providing him with. He didn't impress us at all. Any time you visit a fire station, you should expect to get some good information to write down. Also, if he didn't feel it was important to bring pen and paper, how is he going to be at work when he has to think and act on his own at times? Gee Chief, I didn't think it was that important, so I didn't do it! Yeah right.

Dress appropriately.

Don't be the candidate that comes into the station in a tank top, shorts, and flip-flops. Don't be like many of the other candidates that do that. Remember that you don't want to be a clone. You want to stand out from the other candidates in a positive way. For the men: a simple polo style or button-down shirt is appropriate for a top (try to stay away from t-shirts); khakis or even clean (not distressed looking) jeans are appropriate for pants, and for shoes, you can wear any type of casual, clean, polished, and closed-toe shoes (no sandals). For the women: an appropriate shirt would be something tasteful, and non-revealing; clean and presentable pants; and for your shoes, you can wear any type of casual, clean, polished, and closed-toe shoes (no sandals). You don't have to be as formal as you would for an oral interview, but you do have to dress appropriately and not too casual.

Why? Because you never know who you're going to meet at the fire station, and where you'll see them again. I remember the time I was in a T-shirt, shorts, and tennis shoes visiting a fire station. I thought I was cool and everything until the Fire Chief walked in and the Captain introduced me to him. I found out later from the Captain that the Chief likes everyone in the department to always where their uniform because he is into a professional image. As luck would have it, I ended up getting a Chief's Interview. Unfortunately I was so nervous when I went in there because of how I was dressed when I first met him, that I did not do as good as I could have. Yes, there are those that say that they are not going to be someone they are not and that the Chief should take them as they are. Keep thinking in that form or fashion and I bet your chances of getting hired will greatly decrease. It's not what they can do for you - it's what you can do for them.

Do not overstay your welcome.

You should expect to be there anywhere from 30 minutes to maybe an hour or so. Any more than that is eating into their daily routine. Believe it or not, many fire departments do not sit in the chairs all day waiting for the bell to go off. They have to do hydrant testing, training, physical fitness, apparatus and facility maintenance, fire prevention inspections, public education details, and of course, go on emergency and non-emergency responses. The more time they spend with you, the less time they have to do those things. Don't get me wrong; I understand the importance of meeting with firefighter candidates during a testing process, and I will happily put aside some of those details to help someone out. I've even had candidates come into the workout room and pull up a chair while I ran on the treadmill, just so I could get my workout in.

Do not wait until the last minute to stop by the fire station.

If I had a dollar for every candidate that stopped by at 8:00 p.m. the night before his or her interview, desperate for our assistance, I would be a rich person. What made them wait so long? Leave yourself plenty of preparation time in advance. Showing up at the last minute only proves to us that you have poor time management and/or organizational skills.

If you find yourself doing more talking then listening, you're probably digging yourself a hole!

You need to be a sponge. Ask a question, and then let them answer. Remember this is not a time to brag about how great you are or let them know how crazy the department would be by not hiring you.

If you get a good vibe from the crew that you've been talking with, ask them if you could schedule a mock oral interview with them at a later date (don't forget to also bring desert then).

Mock orals can be tricky if you get people assisting you that have not been on an oral panel for years or have very little experience in the way of assisting candidates. One thing you should be asking at the station is if any of them have sat on the oral panels recently. If they have, then you might see if they would be willing to give you a mock oral. Take it for what it is worth - someone's opinion. Just remember that everyone has opinions, not one opinion is necessarily right, and you can learn something from everyone.

Do not forget to thank the crew for taking the time to assist you.

Even a simple thank-you note mailed to them after the visit is a nice gesture that would allow them to remember you in a positive light (unless you were a bumbling idiot and the thank you note keeps your name in their heads forever!).

When you are leaving, ask the Captain and the crew if there are any other stations they would suggest you stop by as well.

On that same note, ask them if there are any other individuals within the fire department that they would recommend you talk to as well. When I have high quality candidates stop by and ask me this questions, I try and point them to people that have been recently hired as well as people I know have sat on past oral boards (because they have a good idea of what they liked and disliked in the candidates that they felt to be the best candidates).

Last, but not least, remember this little nugget.

You are in the spotlight 100% of the time you are at the fire station. Don't let your guard down! The entire time you are there, the crewmembers are informally testing you. They might ask you a question such as "why do you want to work for us?" or "tell us about yourself." Make sure that you have good answers to those questions (which you should already have because you have been practicing and rehearsing for your oral interviews, haven't you?). If you just keep in mind that visiting fire stations can either help your outcome or hurt your outcome, you should be able to make that positive first impression (the impression that will potentially last your entire career).

Visiting fire stations is a very critical part of the firefighter testing process. Make that positive first impression, and you increase your chances of success!

Ride Along Etiquette

Getting the opportunity to ride along with a fire department, police department, or ambulance crew is an incredible privilege. You get the chance to gain an inside look at their internal operations as well as meet a great bunch of people that can help assist you in your pursuit of your dream career. The impression you make when you participate in a ride along can help your chances or hurt your chances of getting a job with that agency. Many people do a ride along for the fun and excitement of it, and don't have the desire (or maybe ability) to ever work with that agency. I've always had the desire to do a ride along with both the San Francisco Fire Department and the Fire Department New York. While I don't see myself switching fire departments at this point in my career, I still think it would be fun to do and awesome to be able to look back in later years and say I've had the chance to do that.

First of all, you might wonder how you would go about arranging a ride along with an agency. The easiest way is to call the main administration number (do some research on their website) and see if they even allow someone to do a ride along. Not every agency allows people to ride along on their field apparatus. Once you find an agency that allows ride alongs, then you need to find out the parameters of their ride along program. Some departments only allow you to be there for a certain time frame (such as daytime hours only). Some departments only allow you to do one ride along per year. Most departments have a dress code for you to abide by. Those are the main things to worry about. What I suggest is to build a data base of sorts where you can list all of the agencies in your area that offer ride alongs, and what their requirements and/or parameters are (because you might want to do more than one ride along).

Many agencies do not allow ride alongs during the testing process, so if you want to do one, you better have prepared well in advance of the testing process. I guess they either don't want candidates to get an unfair advantage by doing one, or they don't want the crews to be burdened by having to babysit someone. As a ride along, you should always bear in mind that you are trying to earn the privilege of calling yourself a firefighter. When you become a probationary firefighter, you will have to be focusing all of your efforts on this while you are on duty. If this attitude is developed now, it will make your life easier throughout your career.

Now that you've been assigned to a unit to ride along with, here are some suggestions to make sure you get off on the right foot and leave them with a positive first impression:

1. Whenever you are personally asked to do a ride along with a crew, take them up on that offer. It is not uncommon to be visiting fire stations or meeting firefighters and have them extend an offer to you to come on down and do a ride along either then or in the future.

2. You are a guest in someone else's firehouse. You need to behave like a considerate guest – otherwise you will wear out your welcome very quickly!

3. Go on every response that you can. At 0300 hours, don't say, "I'm tired" or "I've already been on that type of call." Once you're hired you can't be selective, so don't be selective now.

4. There is a camaraderie that exists when a company has been together awhile. Sometimes the bantering and joking gets rough. Get used to it! You'll have to earn your way into this group. Be careful and go slow or you'll create resentment.

5. Use discretion when sitting in the recliners. You'll have plenty of chair time after you're hired and off of probation.

6. Work out only if invited to do so. Remember, you are a guest.

You can work out on your own time or at the gym. Try to use your time more wisely.

7. Know your apparatus inventory. The chances are your company officer will use you as a gofer on your first runs. If you don't know where things are on the apparatus, you are worthless to the crew. Opening and closing every compartment on the emergency scene because you don't remember where something is stored is embarrassing and makes you look stupid!

8. Remember, the public is always watching you. Even though you probably have non-fire department related apparel on, you are still considered to be a representative of that fire department (or other agency) – for the most part, the public doesn't know the difference.

9. Pay your station food fund before being asked. At the start of the shift, ask the crew how much your share will be for the day. Don't expect them to break large bills, always attempt to have exact change. Many departments don't allow banking on duty; so don't ask them to stop at an ATM for you. Also, don't forget to chip in for the daily house dues. Daily house dues are usually a few dollars a day to cover the newspaper, coffee, and other miscellaneous items.

10. You should be the last person to sit down to eat, the last person to fill your plate, and the first person done eating. Always be the first person to start performing kitchen cleanup. Don't immediately jump up to do the dishes when you are done; many crews like to let their dinner settle and perform "team-bonding." Wait for a "cue" from the other firefighters to start cleaning up.

11. If you are not a great cook, don't volunteer to cook. Always have a few good meals that you can whip up with minimal prep time and minimal cost. Most firefighters want to keep lunch and dinner to $10.00 or less per day. It is always better to have extra food than to run out! Don't plan on spending all day preparing for the night's meal unless you're a paid firefighter. If you're not cooking, volunteer to assist with dinner preparation and with setting the table.

12. No matter what you are doing, keep a positive, happy attitude while doing it. Remember, they don't have to have you there.

13. The phones are not for you. Stay away from them except when necessary. Most stations have an official business line and a second "private line" or "back line" that firefighters use for personal use. Don't answer it unless instructed to do so. If you do answer it, an appropriate greeting would be "good morning (afternoon, evening), station #2, ride along Jones, how may I assist you?"

14. If you have a cell phone on you or with you, PUT IT ON VIBRATE or leave it in your vehicle! Also, do not answer it while on an apparatus or in the middle of doing something on a call, or at the fire station. It is rude and disrespectful. Unless an immediate family member has died or has been seriously injured, do not be tempted to use your phone or feel like you have to immediately call back everyone who calls you. That is what voice mail is for, and your time off is for.

15. Do not access the station computer to check your email or surf the Internet. Wait until you go home. If you bring a laptop computer, don't plan on using the department phone lines to access the Internet. If you have to, use a wireless Internet connection. Even that is pushing it. A laptop is appropriate for doing homework, but I don't even recommend bringing one in due to the lack of station security.

16. Be polite and respectful to everyone. It is a small world and you never know when and where you might interact with that person in your future.

17. Address all company officers and chief officers by rank. They earned it; you should respect it.

18. Assist the individuals that are on duty that day. Don't wait for them to ask you to assist them. If you see someone doing something, ask him or her if you can assist; especially if it is something you have never done or seen before.

19. If you don't know how or when to use something, ask one of the firefighters to show you. This can include station maintenance,

apparatus maintenance, or apparatus/equipment usage. Don't wait until it is a life or death situation to tell someone "I don't know how to use this tool." You should have solved that problem the minute you encountered the equipment on rig checkout.

20. Either bring a homemade dessert in for the crewmembers (such as chocolate chip cookies) or offer to buy something at the store for them (round, not square ice cream – unless it is Breyers, the good stuff; pies, etc.). Although it is not required, remember that you are a guest for the day and that nothing says that you have to be there for the day. Having a ride along with a crew for the day can be very stressful on the crew because there is now an outsider watching every move they make.

21. You are at the fire station to learn; so learn! Listen; don't talk. I've heard lots of comments from firefighters about "know it all" ride alongs. Don't say, "at the academy we did it this way," or "at the other station they do it this way." Remember, you are there to do it their way. Be flexible and adaptable, there are many right ways to do things. Remember; when in Rome, do as the Romans do.

22. Don't tell people what you know or what you can do. Let your actions speak for themselves.

Doing ride alongs with various fire departments was an eye opening experience for me because it really convinced me that this was the career I wanted to get into. Plus, it allowed me something to talk about when I was asked the question "how have you prepared yourself to become a firefighter?" Before I took the Captain's promotional exam at my department, I went up to our dispatch center and spent about four hours performing a "sit-along" with a couple of dispatchers. That really opened my eyes to how tough of a job the dispatchers have. I sincerely believe their job can be more stressful than our job much of the time. Communications was an area I had a lot of questions about, so by doing that sit along, I was able to get those questions answered. It also provided me with an understanding of what they do, which will allow me to better interact with them on the radio. It also gave me something to add to my answer when I was asked in the oral interview, "how have I prepared myself for the position of Captain." How many other candidates did what I did? None that I was aware of. It was something that might have made me stand out from my competitors.

I highly recommend to anyone wanting a career in the fire department, the police department, and or the EMS world, to go out and do a ride along with the various agencies - big departments, small departments, etc. Expose yourself to a variety of agencies so that you can see what might work best for you and your career. Follow the suggestions I have provided and you increase your chances of leaving the crew with a positive and lasting first impression!

Researching A Fire Department

Conducting research relating to a fire department, and when a fire department will be accepting applications is a critical element in relation to getting a job as a firefighter. Don't expect a fire department to call you when it is time to accept applications for the position of firefighter! You have to be prepared for that application-filing period to ensure success. One way to be prepared is to develop your firefighter candidate research binder and start obtaining valuable information that can make a positive difference in your pursuit of becoming a firefighter.

On pages 193 through 199, you will find a sample template I suggest that you use. I feel it covers a majority of the information that a candidate would need to be one of the best-prepared candidates.

Sample F.D. Information Template

Name: _____

Address: _____

Website url: _____

Facebook: Yes/No   Twitter: Yes/No   If Yes, Twitter handle: _____

Business Phone #: _____

Year established: _____

Cities / Communities served:

_____

Population Served: _____

Square Miles: _____

I.S.O. Rating: _____

CFAI Accredited? _____

    If accredited, year of first Accreditation? _____

    If accredited, year of next Accreditation? _____

Level of EMS provided: _____

    ALS Engines? _____   ALS Trucks? _____

    Other ALS apparatus? _____

Ambulance transport provided by: _____

Dispatching services provided by: _____

Total Calls last year: _____

EMS Responses (# and % of total): _____

Fire Responses (# and % of total): _____

Other: _____

I.A.F.F. Union Local #: _____

Union President Name: _____

Union website url: _____

F.D. Budget: _____

Primary sources of F.D. Revenue: _____

Primary sources of F.D. Expenditures: _____

Apparatus Information:

 # Of Fire Stations: _____

 # Of Engines: _____   **# Of Reserve Engines:** _____

 # Of Trucks: _____   **# Of Reserve Trucks:** _____

 # Of Ambulances: _____   # ALS: _____ # BLS: _____

 # Of Rescue Companies: _____   # Of Battalions: _____

 # Of Haz Mat units: _____   Other specialized apparatus?

_____

Any cross-staffed apparatus?

_____

Apparatus Manufacturers Used:

_____

Staffing (Personnel on each apparatus):

Engines: _____   Trucks: _____   Rescues: _____

Other: _____

Minimum # of personnel on duty each shift: _____

Personnel Information:

of Uniformed personnel: _____ # of Civilian personnel: _____

Name of Fire Chief: _____

Of Deputy Chiefs: _____

    Names of each/ Divisions each Deputy Chief oversees:

    _____

    _____

    _____

Of Assistant Chiefs: _____

    Names of each / Divisions each Assistant Chief oversees:

    _____

    _____

    _____

Of Division Chiefs: _____

    Names of each / Divisions each Division Chief oversees:

    _____

    _____

    _____

 # Of Battalion Chiefs: _____   Shift: _____   40-hour: _____

 # Of Captains: _____   Shift: _____   40-hour: _____

 # Of Lieutenants: _____   Shift: _____   40-hour: _____

 # Of Engineers: _____   Shift: _____   40-hour: _____

 # Of Firefighters: _____   Shift: _____   40-hour: _____

Volunteer or Reserve Firefighter program? _____

    # Of Volunteer/Reserve Firefighters: _____

    Requirements to be a Volunteer/Reserve: _____

    Their role: _____

Explorer or Cadet Firefighter program? _____

    # Of Explorer or Cadet Firefighters: _____

    Requirements to be an Explorer/Cadet: _____

    Their role: _____

 # Of Fire Prevention Bureau personnel: _____

    Name/Rank of Fire Marshal: _____

    # Of Assistant Fire Marshals: _____

    # Of Senior Deputy Fire Marshals: _____

    # Of Deputy Fire Marshals: _____

    # Of Fire Inspectors: _____

    Other ranks within the Fire Prevention Bureau:

    _____

    Are the Prevention personnel sworn or civilian? _____

Fire Investigation duties handled by: _____

Public Education duties handled by: _____

Wage & Benefit Information:

Type of Retirement System: _____

    Retirement Formula: _____

    Retirement contributions: Paid by F.D.? _____ Paid by employee? _____

Medical Benefits:

    Paid by F.D.? _____ Paid by employee? _____

Compensation:

    Entry salary: _____

    Top step Firefighter salary: _____

    Years to top step: _____ EMT incentive? _____

    Paramedic incentive? _____ Uniform Allowance? _____

    Other specialty pay: _____

Type of shift worked: _____

 # Of Vacation days received: _____

Other benefits: _____

Employment Information:

Personnel / Human Resource Office Location:

_____

    Phone Number: _____ Job Line Number: _____

    City / County web site: _____

Do they accept interest cards for Firefighter? _____

Firefighter Testing process consists of (check all that apply):

Written test (what type?): _____

Oral interview: _____

Physical ability test (or CPAT): _____

Background investigation: _____

Chief's interview: _____

Medical Examination: _____

Polygraph: _____

Psychological Examination: _____

Other: _____

Minimum Requirements for Firefighter:

_____

Last tested for Firefighter: _____

 # Of candidates hired off last list: _____

Next Firefighter test? _____

Present # of vacancies: _____   **Projected # of future vacancies:** _____

Length of Academy: _____

Length of probation: _____

Do they tend to release Firefighters during the Academy or probationary period (if so, why)?

_____

<u>Miscellaneous:</u>

Major Target Hazards: _____

_____

Type of area served by the fire department: _____

Future stations planned? _____

Future projects or programs planned by the department? _____

_____

Response Assignments for various types of calls:

EMS response: _____

Vehicle accident: _____

Vehicle accident with rescue: _____

Vegetation fire: _____

Smoke inside a structure: _____

Fire inside a structure: _____

First alarm assignment: _____

Second alarm assignment: _____

Third alarm assignment: _____

Fourth-alarm assignment: _____

Haz Mat response: _____

Rescue (non-vehicle accident): _____

Other types of responses: _____

Busiest Station: _____   **Busiest Unit / # of calls last year:** _____

NOTE: If you want to a cleaner copy of the above Sample F.D. Information template, you can either email me at sprziborowski@aol.com or visit my website at www.code3firetraining.com and click on the FREE STUFF link to locate a copy of the template.

To actually do some research on when a fire department will be next accepting applications, where do you start? I believe you should do an all encompassing approach that will include using the internet, calling up the fire department administrative offices to see if you can arrange a fire station visit, calling up the city personnel department, stopping by a fire station, and stopping by the City Hall (or other similar administrative offices of the municipality, county, state, or federal agency you are applying for).

I provided above a sample template to use that contained information on a fire department that I feel will be very relevant and useful in performing your research. You probably saw that template and asked yourself, "How am I going to obtain all of the necessary information?" Obtaining that information will be the focus of the next few pages. Think of yourself as a detective trying to piece together a crime. Instead, you will be piecing together the pieces that will complete the puzzle of pursuing your dream of becoming a firefighter!

In addition to the above template, when talking to the firefighters at your local fire station, ask them questions such as:

- How does your department differ from other departments?
- What do you like about your fire department?
- What do you think could be improved about your fire department?
- Can you give me a tour of the fire station and the apparatus?
- Is there anything you would recommend I do to increase my chances at becoming a firefighter?
- Do you recommend anyone else within your department for me to talk to, such as recently hired personnel or personnel I may benefit from meeting?

Don't just rely on one fire station; talk to firefighters at other fire stations in your city, as well as other fire departments (each fire department is slightly different from the next one) as you'll realize quickly each department and even each station at times may have it's own unique culture, good, bad or indifferent.

Additional information can also be found in the previous section titled "How To Properly Present Yourself During A Fire Station Visit."

Creating Your Candidate
Research Binder

If you are thinking that you are getting in over your head, then sit down and take a deep breath. Rome wasn't built in a day, and odds are you are not going to become a firefighter in a day either. Patience is a virtue. All of this research you perform now is going to be valuable information that will assist you in some form or fashion. Where do we start? Now that you have this nice binder, what are you going to do with it? Hopefully use it! There are many ways you can obtain information to "fill in the blanks."

Here are my suggestions to assist you in the process of filling in the blanks for each of the fire departments you are planning to research (remember we are using the template I showed you on the previous pages, or something similar):

#1: Searching the Internet.

If you can't find what you're looking for on a website links page such as firehouse.com, you can use a search engine such as Google, yahoo, etc. Those would all be excellent choices. Once there, you would type in such specific words as City of Oakland or Oakland Fire Department. Personally I would start off with the City web site first. Why? Because that is usually the easiest to find, and they also have links to City Departments such as the Fire Department and Personnel / Human

Resources. Once at the City web site, I would bookmark the City web site for future access, and additionally bookmark the Fire Department web site. That way I would have both to reference from.

#2: I'm at the City or County website, what do I now do?

Go directly to the Personnel / Human Resources section. This can be found usually by looking under CITY DEPARTMENTS or JOBS or EMPLOYMENT or CITY HALL or something similar. Once there, this section will allow you to see if there are firefighter vacancies. Chances are, there are not. That's ok, you shouldn't have gotten your hopes up - you are in this for the long haul, and are using this information to better prepare yourself. If you happen to find a fire department is testing by chance, then consider yourself lucky. Besides current job openings, you can see if they take interest cards (which allow you to be notified when they are recruiting for a certain position, such as firefighter). You can also copy down their address, their business phone number, their 24-hour job hotline, and any other information you feel valuable. *DON'T FORGET TO BOOKMARK THIS PAGE FOR FUTURE REFERENCE!*

#3: After visiting the Personnel / Human Resource section, what information should I obtain next?

Now it is time to navigate to the FIRE DEPARTMENT portion of the website. Most fire departments have websites, and they can usually be accessed in the same fashion as the Personnel / Human Resource office. Just go under CITY DEPARTMENTS or PUBLIC SAFETY and click on FIRE DEPARTMENT. Some fire departments have a wealth of information to offer and some have a one-page home page that lists virtually no information that it makes you wonder why they even bothered. Some websites will allow you to complete much of your template just by visiting the website. *DON'T FORGET TO BOOKMARK THIS PAGE FOR FUTURE REFERENCE!*

#4: What happens if I still don't have all of the blanks of my template filled in?

I would suggest stopping by the fire department headquarters, since they will possibly have brochures or other information to provide you with, as well as knowledge of when there might be another firefighter examination. They might even have a person in charge of recruitment you could talk to or a firefighter working at the headquarters who could answer some of your questions. Once at fire headquarters, I would ask them if they could give you a list of addresses for each of their fire stations (many times you can download this information from the fire department website). I would also ask them for the business phone numbers of the fire stations so you could call the station Captain to set up an appointment. I would also ask them such information as:

- Do you know when you are going to test for firefighter again?
- When did you last test for firefighter?
- How many firefighters did you hire off the last list?
- What are your qualifications to take the firefighter test?
- Do you take interest cards?
- When should I contact you to find out more information?

#5: Headquarters or the Administrative Offices was helpful, but I still haven't obtained all of the necessary information.

Now it is time to start visiting fire stations. Hopefully you have called to make an appointment, and are not just dropping by. Most firefighters are usually eager to talk to future firefighters, but not necessarily at a moment's notice. Most firefighters usually have busy schedules during the day in between running calls, and you stopping by might not always be at the best time. Even if you weren't able to make an appointment (because you didn't know the phone number), I would suggest stopping by a local pie shop and bringing a nice pie (homemade works too). This is to thank them for taking valuable time away from their duties, and ask them if you can talk now, or if it would better, could you set up an appointment for another time or day. That would usually work. Bring your binder with your template and be ready to fill in the blanks. Don't overstay your welcome and thank them on the way out.

#6: Keeping track of information and your progress.

Many times, you will need to use multiple ways to fill in the information for each fire department. It might require you to visit city hall, visit a fire station, view their website, and maybe phone the fire department headquarters. Just like you want to back up any important computer files, or leave copies of valuable documents in a safety deposit box, I would think you would want to keep track of your progress. A good way to track your progress is by using the fire department information templates you have already produced for each fire department. Since the backs of those pages are probably blank, here is a good location to list such information as:

- Date you visited or phoned.
- Method of contact (phone, in-person, website, etc.).
- Information you obtained.
- Person(s) you spoke with (you never know when you might need to talk to that person again).
- When to call back or stop by again (this information would then be transferred to your personal calendar to list your action plan / to do items).

You've Started Researching Fire Departments, What Next?

Don't think you're done now! Just because you have filled in the blanks on the previous pages doesn't mean you can stop! Consider this a work-in-progress! Now that you have obtained some valuable information to assist you in the process of becoming a firefighter, it is time to put that information to work. The information you obtain by researching a fire department is invaluable. Why? Because this is where you are going to set yourself up for success by planning out a course of action to find out when those fire departments you spent time researching, are going to accept applications again!

Here is where I would put 12 blank pieces of paper – one for each month of the year. On the top of each page, I would write out each of the 12 months in order, starting with January. If you have a calendar program on your computer, or have enough computer skills to get you in trouble, feel free to make a calendar that way. Otherwise plain paper will work.

Here is where you will make any notes to you of importance. Items I would include here would be tentative or actual dates of any phases of the testing process I might be involved in (written exam, physical ability exam, oral interview, etc.) and any information that I think would be important to act on either within that month or on a specific date. You will find that when you call a personnel office to ask them when they will be testing next for firefighter, a lot of times they will tell you "not now, however, why don't you call us back in March." That would be something important to list on the March page, to ensure you don't miss out on a valuable opportunity.

This section can also be used for tracking any goals or objectives you might have, whether it is recertifying your EMT, renewing your CPR, applying for paramedic school, completing your two-year degree, etc.

If you think this is a waste of time, then so be it. This method worked for me, and I truly believe in being proactive in life, especially when it comes to controlling your own destiny and plotting out your course of action to get you through life. Nobody is going to lead you by the hand when it comes to getting that firefighter badge. It is a very competitive process, and many candidates get discouraged and never achieve that dream. Don't let your self become one of those. A little research now will go along way in the future.

An important thing to remember is that researching fire departments is not just to let you know when they will be accepting applications. It is to better prepare yourself for oral interview questions such as how have you prepared yourself, why do you want to work for our fire department, what do you know about our fire department, etc. If you have done your homework, then you are going to have more ammunition to better answer the question.

**Remember – Don't Just Prepare For The
Test… Prepare For The Position!**

About the Author

Steve Prziborowski is a Deputy Chief with the Santa Clara County Fire Department (Los Gatos, CA), where he has served since 1995 in the following positions: Firefighter/Engineer-Paramedic, Fire Captain, Training Captain, Operations Captain, Battalion Chief, Battalion Chief/EMS Coordinator and now Deputy Chief overseeing Training, EMS, Emergency Preparedness, Community Education, the Volunteer Division and the Explorer Program. Steve has been in the fire service since 1992 when he began his career as an Associate Advisor with the Alameda Fire Department's Fire Explorer program, progressing to a position as a Student Firefighter with the Oakland Fire Department (a work experience program through Chabot College), and then as a paid-call Firefighter and paid-call Firefighter/Paramedic with the Elk Grove Fire Department prior to getting hired full-time with Santa Clara County Fire.

Steve has been an Adjunct Faculty member at Chabot College (Hayward, CA) since 1993. Steve spent seven years as the EMT Program Director and Primary Instructor, and almost five years as the Fire Technology Coordinator, and is currently the primary instructor for the Introduction to Fire Protection course. In addition to maintaining the Chabot College Fire Technology Program website – www.chabotfire. com, Steve also teaches oral interview preparation for the Firefighter 1 Academy.

Steve is recognized as a leading fire service instructor, was selected as the 2008 California Fire Service Instructor of the year and is a contributing editor to Firehouse.com. He is a Former President of the Northern California Training Officers Association, has completed the Executive Fire Officer Program at the National Fire Academy, and has received Chief Fire Officer Designation through the Commission on Professional Credentialing. He is a state-certified Chief Officer and Master Instructor, has earned a Master's degree in Emergency Services Administration, as well as a Bachelor's Degree in Criminal Justice and an Associate's Degree in Fire Technology.

Steve is currently a Program Planning Committee member for the International Association of Fire Chiefs Fire Rescue International Conference, as well as a member of a number of fire service organizations and associations. Steve has instructed, mentored and coached thousands of fire service personnel around the Country (current and future) of all ranks from Volunteer/Reserve Firefighter up to Fire Chief. He is a regular speaker and presenter at fire service events and conferences around the Country such as Firehouse Events, FDIC and the Fresno Symposium, and has authored numerous articles in all of the leading fire service publications such as Fire Engineering, Firehouse, Fire Rescue Magazine and Fire Chief, just to name a few.

Steve has also published two other books, "Reach For The Firefighter Badge," and "How To Excel At Fire Department Promotional Exams."

To inquire about seminar or conference
presentations, please visit my websites at

www.chabotfire.com

and

www.code3firetraining.com

Made in the USA
San Bernardino, CA
24 September 2018